NEEDLEPOINT
AND PATTERN

NEEDLEPOINT AND PATTERN

Themes and Variations

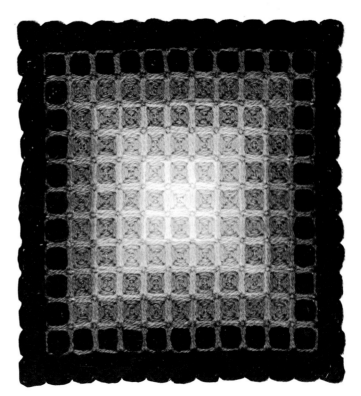

GLORIA
KATZENBERG

MACMILLAN PUBLISHING CO., INC.
NEW YORK
COLLIER MACMILLAN PUBLISHERS
LONDON

To my father

Charles M. Balder

Macmillan Publishing Co., Inc.
866 Third Avenue, New York, N.Y. 10022
Collier-Macmillan Canada Ltd.

Library of Congress Cataloging in Publication Data

Katzenberg, Gloria.
  Needlepoint and pattern.

  Bibliography: p.
  1. Canvas embroidery—Patterns. I. Title.
TT778.C3K37   746.4'4   72-92450
ISBN 0-02-560810-X

Second Printing 1975

Printed in the United States of America

ACKNOWLEDGMENTS

My thanks to everyone who had a part in this book: my mother, Mrs. Charles M. Balder, who stitched many of the patterns, and Vicki Mitchell, who typed the manuscript.

And to the following:

Mary Rhodes, the author of *Ideas for Canvas Work,* published by B. T. Batsford of London, who gave permission to use the Rhodes stitch and provided a diagram of the French knot. Special thanks, too, for her hospitality during my visit to her class for advanced embroiderers in Eltham, England.

Leonard L. Greif, Jr., who photographed the stitches and the finished needlepoint articles in the book.

Susan Katzenberg, for her photograph of the cane bench on page 134.

Mayfair May who kept a cluttered house in amazing order through it all.

Robert M. Goldman, for many helpful gestures.

The late Mariska Karasz, my friend, who first introduced me to the idea of art through stitches.

My editor, Amanda Vaill . . . she knows why.

Mary Adler, Betty Gelfand, Adele Levi, Margery Peyton, Louis Gartner of Bergdorf Goodman; Betty Malmud of Needlepoint Corner; and Nanette Greif and my mother for the loan of their wonderful needlepoint for this book.

Most of all, to Herbert M. Katzenberg, my husband, for a long list of aids, suggestions, and supports.

In this rare art yet here they may diserne
Some things to teach them if they list to learne.
        —John Taylor, *The Needles Excellency,* 1640

CONTENTS

PREFACE

There is a bit of the designer lurking deep inside all of us, which can, with some direction and a natural urge for expression, make an enchanting contribution to needlepoint design. I hope my book will appeal to the fascinated beginner and to the seemingly sated expert ready for new directions and fresh enticements. My designs should help you to visualize the way creative ideas were developed stage by stage into design reality. They should serve as starting points and stimuli to your own powers of invention. It won't be long before you advance to higher and higher levels of creativity and control of techniques.

A unique result in needlepoint—as in other arts and handcrafts—is more likely to occur when you, the craftsman, are also the designer. Design and work when done by one hand achieve a unity, a spontaneity, and a personal imprint difficult to realize in any other way.

With a dazzling array of colors and stitches, the tools and materials of embroidery, needlepoint, and other media, you can realize your design fantasies. The basics of needlepoint design are presented here. Learn the techniques with the understanding that they should not be restrictive or inhibiting to design. Use them to get the effects you want, and when you feel confident that you have a grasp of fine craftsmanship, depart from them. Then you will be closer to the realm of the artist—reaching beyond conventional limits of form, color, and texture.

Historically, needlepoint flourished as a functional and decorative art of great charm, imagination, and flawless craftsmanship. Different countries and eras have left us a heritage to which we can add today's sensibilities, tastes, subject matter, and sophisticated technology. I will try to show you how to use the lessons of the past while stressing the excitement of today's discoveries—which, after all, will make up the valued inheritance of tomorrow.

PART I

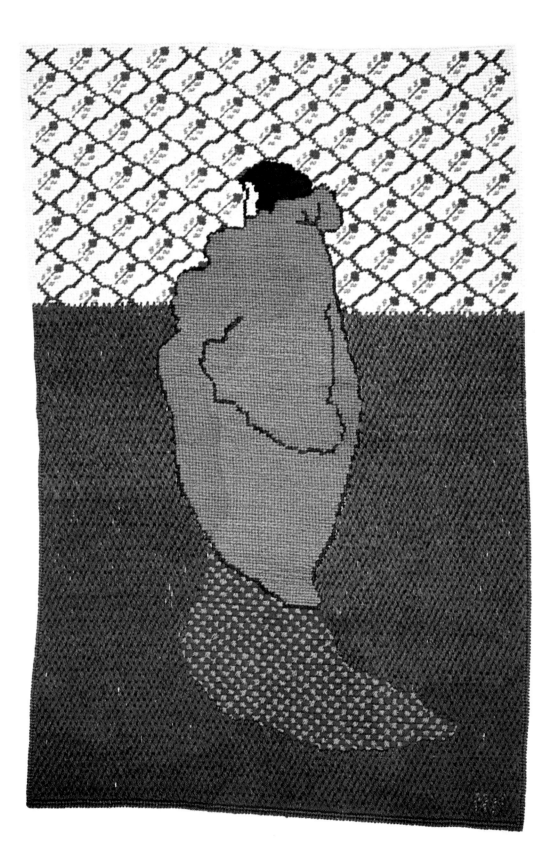

1 NEEDLEPOINT AND PATTERN

What began a few years ago as a needlepoint renaissance has become a fever of activity in the United States. Everyone is trying it: young and old, male and female alike. In a recent exhibit of needlework, held at Woodlawn Plantation in Virginia, an entire room was devoted to needlework by men. A sign was posted above the door, bearing the whimsical title, "Men's Room."

The manufacturers of tea and Kleenex offer needlepoint projects as bonuses to customers willing to fill out a coupon on the package. Community centers and museums are offering courses in needlepoint. The elderly find it easy to master and are using it to help support themselves. The needlepoint festival has become a most successful way of fund raising because it brings everybody out. At board meetings hardly a pair of idle hands can be seen, except, of course, those of the speaker.

Needlepoint has been called a therapy and an addiction. Actually, it is an art of great age—useful, beautiful, soothing, and fun to do. And it has so many advantages: It requires no special workroom or elaborate equipment. It is portable. When the work is finished, no massive cleanup is necessary. The stitches are easy to learn, and the rules are few. And it is enduring.

Why has the art of needlepoint conquered the U.S.A., reaching so many diverse communities? In an age of mass-produced objects and look alikes, there is a yearning for individuality. Creating with one's own hands seems to satisfy that urge. There is the need to transcend the invasion of technology and to bring beauty in all its forms closer. A fireside rug, designed and stitched by you, is a reminder of the joy of creativity and self-expression. And you have an heirloom on your hands!

LADY IN EVENING WRAP

Inspired by an Aubrey Beardsley poster, *Lady* stands against a patterned wallpaper and on a patterned floor. Her hair is a mass of French knots and the skirt of her long dress, showing under the wrap, is still another pattern. This wall hanging is a good example of the compatibility of many patterns worked in a single design. *(Worked by Mrs. Richard Peyton.)*

Needlepoint, also called canvas embroidery, is the art of embellishing the surface of a woven cotton material with stitches and a variety of threads. Worked over the evenly spaced meshes of canvas, the stitches are intended to cover the fabric completely in the form of a design of your own choice. In this sense then, needlepoint is counted stitches on canvas. I refer to painted needlepoint as pictorial design. This book will focus on another facet of needlepoint—a facet in which designs are worked, following few guidelines, directly on perfectly blank canvas. I refer to this facet as *pattern.*

Pattern is simply a form of design using a varied but controlled vocabulary of stitches that are arranged, combined, repeated, and juxtaposed into a decorative scheme. It is in this arranging, not in the laying on of painted forms to be faithfully followed, that the design is born. Color, thread, and texture add further dimensions. Pattern is the geometric division of space or, in our case, canvas. It may be one motif by itself, or it may be the even or uneven repetition of lines, shapes, motifs, colors, and textures. While repetition is basic to pattern and its rhythm pleasing to the eye, tasteful variation saves it from being mechanical and monotonous. The fun and the challenge of making needlepoint patterns depend on the techniques of variation. They are easy to learn and are best explained in the context of the patterns as they appear in the book.

The forms of pattern that surround us in architecture, painting, engraving, and textile go back thousands of years. The sight of a checkerboard, the zigzag, stripe, basketweave, lattice, fish scale, Greek key, lozenge, circle, square, and triangle is second nature to us. These, along with patterns based on natural forms (leaves, flowers, animals, etc.) are easily adapted to design on canvas. The universality of these forms makes them timeless,

ISOLATED GEOMETRIC MOTIFS

I experimented on blank canvas with an assortment of traditional themes—(left to right, top to bottom) the Greek key, the butterfly, the honeycomb, the diamond, the circle, the flower, the square, the zigzag, the triangle, another diamond, the stripe, the fish-scale or scallop, and the spiral—fascinated by how they would work in needlepoint design.

3

and their intriguing relation to needlepoint emerges in the form of traditional, contemporary, provincial, and sophisticated approaches to design.

Most of the patterns are easy to understand. They require no design training. There is no drawing, no transferring, no painting. The pattern is usually set by some elementary counting, either from a graph or from an already worked piece. Most patterns are arranged so that once the outline or first row is correctly set up, the counting is minimal. The rest is the creative and challenging part—inventively filling in stitches, colors, and textures.

I have been intrigued with pattern making and feel that it has not been fully explored as has painted needlepoint design. I hope my readers will delve into *all* types of needlepoint; one kind is not superior to another. Doing your own designing, however, is so much less costly, more fun, and offers more opportunity for self-expression and inventiveness. Pattern and pictorial design, by the way, are quite *simpatico* side by side in the same piece of work. There can be a patterned border around a painted canvas, for example, and pattern is often worked as background for a pictorial design.

The purpose of this book is to celebrate pattern making in needlepoint and offer a varied collection of designs that you can do by yourself. Either work them as they are, down to the last color, or improvise by changing a line, a stitch, a thread, if you feel so inspired. Read the book and enjoy and examine the full-view photographs; you will soon understand how to adapt the patterns and personalize them. Better still, you will become so attuned to the ideals of imagination and improvisation that nothing short of your own designs will satisfy you. Independence and invention are where the real fun is!

BLOCKS

A good example of how exciting a simple repetition of design motifs can be, this pattern is composed of alternating rows of diamonds and squares, with the juxtaposition of the different colors creating an almost three-dimensional effect. The design is easily transposed from photograph to canvas.

SERPENT

The background of the painted paisley serpent is a zigzag pattern in Florentine stitches worked in D.M.C. *mouline spécial* (stranded cotton) and wool. The pattern suggests the undulating movements of the serpent, the background relating to the central motif of the work. The serpent is worked entirely in tent stitches in lustrous cotton providing a textural contrast throughout the design: smooth and shiny against rough and flat. The eye of the serpent is a large glass button, donated by a dear friend, the late Jacqueline Hess.

5

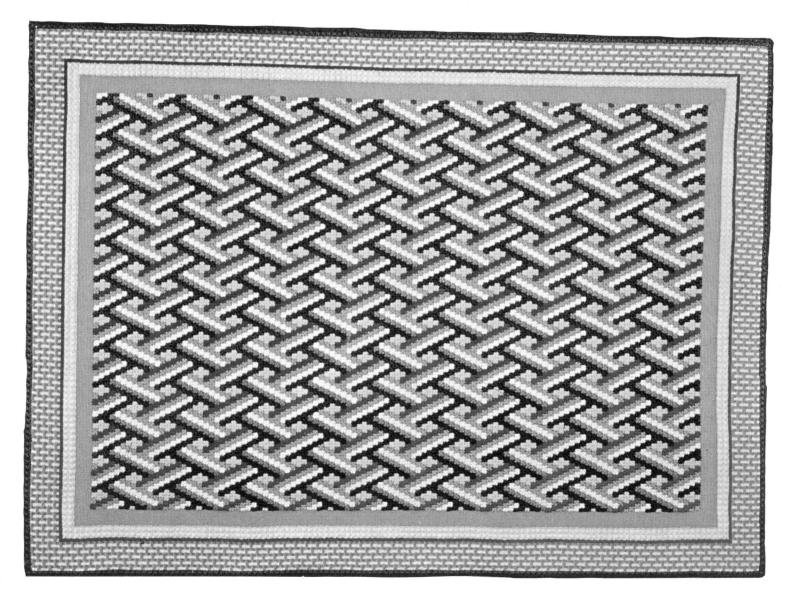

6

2 WHAT'S THE USE OF NEEDLEPOINT?

There is a marvelous interplay of colors, motifs, and stitches in this rug that borrows at least the borders of Oriental rug design. The center of the rug is worked in "Rice Ribbons," an especially textured pattern that is diagonally arranged on the canvas. There are several borders of solid colors, but one border is a second ribboned pattern worked in tent stitches and arranged vertically, echoing the center design. The contrast in direction and in texture of the border and center patterns and their close proximity heightens the interest of the whole design and gives it special vitality. The rug was worked on Number 10 canvas with three threads of Persian yarn—though you may find a fourth thread is necessary to cover the canvas when working rice stitches. (Worked by Mrs. Charles M. Balder.)

THE USES OF NEEDLEPOINT

Needlepoint can be used in engaging ways and has extraordinary adaptability. It adapts to any color, any style, or any period. Whether your home is formal or casual, English, French, Chinese, or American in feeling, your needlepoint can be made to reflect it. Needlepoint is compatible with antiques of any country or period and is especially enhancing to a contemporary, or even ultramodern setting. Many interior designers favor a blend of old and new—antique tables with chairs covered in the fabrics, colors, and textures of today, including today's needlepoint.

Needlepoint makes beautiful rugs: area rugs, fireside rugs, scatter rugs, and stair runners. In the guest bathroom, a tiny needlepoint rug adds a warm, personal touch to what might otherwise be a cold, undistinguished, and impersonal tile floor. A dark narrow hall can be transformed into Versailles by a sophisticated, colorful runner of your own design. Worked in sturdy wool and using suitable stitches, rugs will hold up well under hard wear and tear, and they are easily cleaned by a dry cleaner.

Another group of possible projects includes chair cushions, sofa pillows, footstools, and bench and piano seat covers.

Dining room chairs have been a favorite challenge since Martha Washington stitched her chair seats in a lovely shell motif. Each chair seat does not have to be exactly identical; in fact, they can all be different, but each should relate to the other seats, as well as to the other surroundings in the room. One decorating idea is to use a different pattern on each of the side chairs but to keep the pattern for the host's and hostess' chair the same.

American country chair with cushion worked in scallop pattern with cross-stitches. (See Chapter 8.) *(Worked by Gloria Katzenberg.)*

Antique stool upholstered in colorful *geometric leaves* pattern (See Chapter 6.) *(Worked by Mrs. Jerome Gelfand.)*

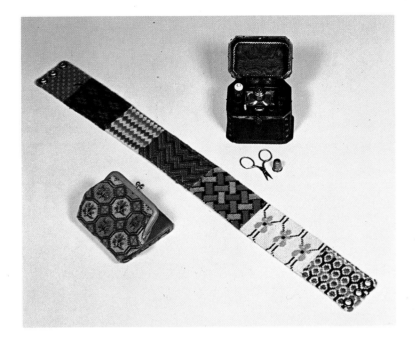

Seven different patterns worked with five different stitches are the foundation of the cinch waist belt shown with a Victorian sewing tool box and a French purse worked in tent stitch pattern. The belt proves how comfortably colors and textures live together. Both belt and purse are mounted in leather to match by professional finishers.

So many choices! Such decisions create quite a pleasant dilemma. Again, do choose a pattern that is in tune with the flavor of your room, whether it be formal, casual, quiet, colorful, or rustic.

When making needlepoint to be used for upholstery, be sure to select the gauge of canvas that fits the chair, bench, or stool to be covered. Not only would a quickpoint canvas (see p. 15) be gross for a Sheraton chair, the canvas would be too bulky to fit into the chair frame. A delicate piece of furniture requires a finer gauge canvas and smaller scale design. Larger canvas is more suitable to heavier chairs, settees, and contemporary pieces. The average loveseat, sofa, or chair can be comfortably covered with either Number 16 or Number 14 mesh canvas.

Needlepoint can brighten your wardrobe, too. The bolero, cummerbund, or belt with buckles or long leather laces are all very popular. An evening vest can be made dressy with a subtle metallic thread or a touch of rayon thread, along with wool. Wool, however, is the most durable of the threads, so use it predominantly, with the other threads as accents. I recently saw an exciting sleeveless, midilength evening coat designed to be worn over velvet pants. It was very colorful and accented with iridescent beads.

All kinds of handbags, from tiny evening bags worked with glass beads to tote bags and hand luggage, are favorite needlepoint projects. Use small-gauge canvas for small items so that finished handbags, wallets, belts, and other accessories can be mounted properly and will not be too bulky. When using antique handbag frames be especially wary in determining that the canvas is fine enough to fit into the channel of the frame.

Here is a list of small, quickly worked articles, pleasing and handy for gifts: small duffel bags, pencil boxes, eyeglass cases, wallets, slippers, checkbook covers, scissors cases, change purses, desk sets, watchbands, book covers, Christmas stockings, and dog collars. Almost any object that can be made of fabric or leather can be made with needlepoint. By all means work a needlepoint tote for your needlepoint at the beach—or for your tennis racket and sneakers.

Here are some other ideas: huge, floppy floor cushions strewn around the hearth are very stylish and provide a cozy way to seat extra guests. A needlepoint backgammon or chess board mounted in Lucite combines the practical and the good-looking; and in the bar, needlepoint can be mounted into a Lucite serving tray. The well-known and adaptable Parsons table can be upholstered all over with needlepoint. A good gift for Grandma is the wall picture frame with windows enough for photos of all the grandchildren. Cornices, drapery ties, letter boxes, needlepoint pictures; mirror frames, as well as address, telephone, and cookbook covers also make cherished gifts. The really ambitious needlepointer can make his own headboard. Wastebaskets, ice-buckets, room dividers, wall hangings, screens, luggage racks, doorstops, jewelry- and cigarette-boxes are still other projects for needlepoint in the home. The most bizarre item may be the needlepoint fly-swatter.

Needlepoint can put your personal stamp on anything you touch. One writer made a *trompe l'oeil* desk top on which appeared covers of magazines she had contributed to. It was bordered by state seals suggesting circulation and was accented with the tools of the art of writing. Another very talented designer and needlepointer, a collector of malachite, covered a tabletop in his own embroidered version of this striking stone. To protect it, he had it covered with a glass top.

COLOR AND USE OF DESIGN

The colors and design of needlepoint for your home should be in tune with the surrounding setting; but don't be afraid to toss in some surprising highlights. Above all, remember that good taste and a bit of restraint are always in order. Don't overdo —partly because too much of any good thing can diminish the effect of its uniqueness.

A patchwork sampler exploring eleven stitches, fourteen patterns, and a variety of shades of rusts and beiges was successful enough to be mounted into a telephone book cover for our study. The design was worked directly on canvas without too much planning, although I did select my low-keyed colors carefully. The division of the design areas is quite asymmetrical, dictated by the scale of stitch and pattern. More space was needed for some than others. Rows of continental stitches outline and separate the different patterns.

Some cotton thread was used to vary the surface along with smooth, rough, large, small, flat, and raised stitches. All the design elements appear integrated and harmonious, including the monogram which was intended as another design motif as well as a signature. I used Number 14 canvas and thicker thread for Florentine stitches than was needed for tent stitches.

A chain pattern in four colors on a plain background worked in tent stitch on Number 12 mono canvas makes an elegant handbag. This bag was worked as four separate pieces—two gussets, the flap, and the body—and then mounted, lined, and trimmed professionally in leather. *(Designed by Louis J. Gartner.)*

11

3 MATERIALS AND TOOLS

CANVAS

Canvas for the needlepointer, like clay for the potter, is merely the vehicle for design. Canvas is usually woven of cotton. Its open spaces or meshes are intended to be completely covered with threads. Stiff and uninspiring by itself, it depends on the craftsman to bring it to life in enchanting ways through the inventive use of stitches, color, threads, and texture.

Canvas comes in different gauges or sizes; it is measured by the number of meshes that are in one inch. The numbers indicate how many stitches it takes to cover one inch of canvas. The higher the number the finer the canvas and vice versa. Fourteen mesh will allow fourteen stitches per inch; ten mesh will allow ten stitches in each inch, and so forth.

There are basically two kinds of needlepoint canvas: single thread and double thread. Single thread, also called mono canvas, has one vertical, or warp, thread that crosses over one horizontal, or weft thread, creating a mesh, or hole, between each intersection. The meshes are uniform in size.

Single-thread canvas is available in white, tan, and yellow. Beginners usually find it easier to count stitches over a single-thread canvas because its meshes are larger than those of double-thread canvas.

Double-thread canvas is also called penelope canvas. It is a weave of two vertical threads crossing over two horizontal threads. Penelope is available only in a light tan, or ecru color, and in white.

Canvas is woven in sizes ranging from a coarse penelope canvas of three meshes per inch to a fine-gauge mono canvas of forty meshes to the inch—which is seldom used today. The most widely

GINGHAM NEEDLEPOINT

Checked gingham takes on a new look with the addition of these little wooden beads, added after the design itself was completed. To begin, work twenty-five stitches to a square in the basketweave stitch, alternating four shades of your favorite color. The pattern is worked on Number 10 canvas with a full strand of Persian yarn. Make sure to center the design so that it ends evenly at the margin lines.

used canvas sizes are Numbers 18, 16, 14, 12, 10, and quickpoint sizes of 7, 5, and 3.

Number 18, 16, and 14 canvases are suitable for slippers, handbags, vests, cummerbunds, pillows, eyeglass cases, doorstops, telephone and address book covers, and many other articles.

Number 10 canvas is useful for rugs, large-scale pillow designs, tennis racket covers, tote bags, wall hangings, and designs not dependent on fine detail or delicacy of scale.

Quickpoint canvas is basically a rug canvas that is also used for wall hangings, pillows, and other accessories. Since it has fewer and larger meshes, it requires thicker threads to cover the mesh and works very quickly into a bold, large-scale design.

Fine canvas is covered by stitches using fine thread. If you plan a design with subtle shading and a lot of detail, you must use a finer canvas: Numbers 18, 16, or 14. Logically, if you work sixteen stitches to the inch, rather than ten, you will be able to develop a more detailed design or motif in a given pattern than if you use a larger mesh canvas.

It is most important, no matter what the size, that the canvas be well covered, but you should accept the fact that sometimes a bit of it will show through the yarn. For this reason, you might consider the tan canvas best for working on some patterns. The tan threads are less obtrusive than the white. For painted designs, my preference is white canvas.

When choosing canvas you must keep in mind its ultimate use. A rug design requires a different gauge than a checkbook cover. In almost all needlework shops you can get good advice and help in choosing the gauge that best suits the scale of your design and the use you plan for the finished article.

Canvas is sold by the yard and usually comes in

14

FLEUR DE LIS #1

The size of your canvas makes an enormous difference in the scale and impact of your design. Here is a fleur de lis worked in four shades of apricot—from pale to turkey red —on Number 14 canvas using two strands of Persian wool yarn.

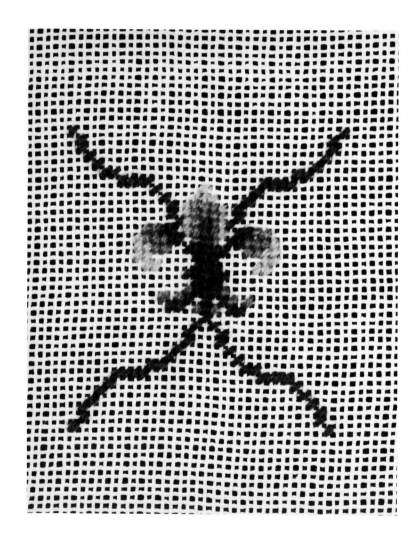

FLEUR DE LIS #2

Here it is on Number 10 canvas using three strands of Persian wool yarn.

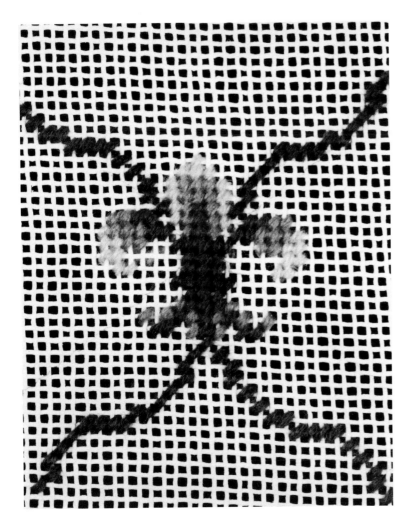

FLEUR DE LIS #3

This is what the same design looks like on double-thread quickpoint canvas, which requires that you use nine full strands, or three full threads, of Persian wool yarn.

widths of 24, 36, 40 and 60 inches. The 60-inch canvas is in Number 10 mesh and mostly used for rugmaking. Like any woven fabric there are selvages or tightly woven edges on either side of the canvas that run vertically with the warp of the canvas. Be sure the selvages are even, tightly woven, and smooth. Reject any canvas with weak, uneven, or knotty places in any part of the canvas. Top-quality canvas is woven of highly polished threads so that the needle and thread can easily pass through the mesh. Canvas is sized with a heavy starchlike finish to give it body and to hold the stitches in place. There is no right or wrong side to canvas. To explore all the potentials of the designs, I purposely used a variety of canvas sizes. The gauge and type of most canvases will be identified, and notes will remind you how different a pattern can be when its scale is changed. A flea can look as large as the American eagle on quickpoint canvas.

THREADS

Today there is an infinite range of threads available—wool, cotton, linen, raffia, chenille, synthetics, metallics, and a glorious range of novelty threads. The main requirement of thread is that it cover the canvas well and that it be sturdy enough to hold up under hard wear. In general, I prefer a durable needlepoint wool for almost everything, and I use other threads in sparing amounts as accents or for textural contrast. Today most wool threads are dyefast and mothproof; they come in a wide range of wonderful colors. You must always test every thread you select for yourself—be sure

16

TWO COLOR SQUARES

Three shades of two different colors are blended together in this mod square design, another checkerboard variation, and the tiny triangles of silver metallic thread in the center of each square gives the whole pattern dash and sparkle. The design is worked here on Number 10 canvas with three strands of Persian yarn and two threads of Silver Goldfingering. The continental stitch is used throughout and should be worked with a very easy tension to prevent stretching the canvas. Work the dark red center stitch of the square in the center of the canvas. With a border of several shades, the design would make a lively rug.

THREADS

This glittering zigzag design underscores the excitement of "special" threads when they are used with plain wool yarn. Gobelin stitches of deep lavender, metallic Goldfingering yarn appear between areas of Florentine stitches worked in variegated knitting yarn shaded from white to deep purple. The latter distributes itself unevenly, with different shades falling in varied positions on the canvas, so it is especially fun to work with, as well as unusual to look at. It was worked on Number 16 canvas.

of proper coverage and durability, and see how it works for you. Ask for advice about each one.

When stitching, be careful not to pull threads too tightly or let them twist as each stitch is made. In fact, it is a good idea to let the needle and thread hang down loosely every now and then; the thread can untwist itself. Keep your stitching tension easy —too much tension tends to pull the canvas out of shape and also causes the canvas threads to show through the yarn. Too little tension will mean uneven and sloppy stitches, but it is better to work loose than tight.

Some threads both cover canvas and hold up well, whereas some very decorative and beautiful threads are very fragile—but because of their

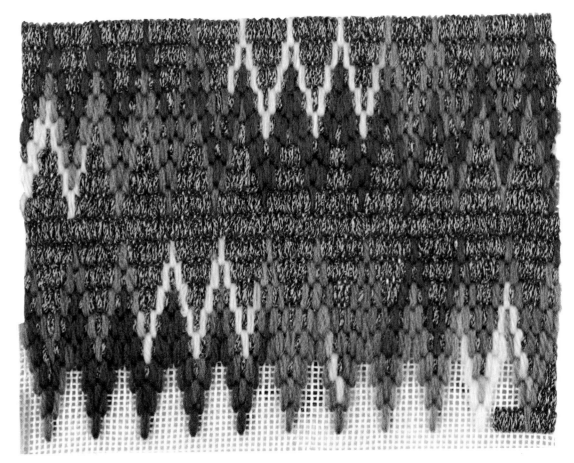

beauty or their superb decorative quality, I wouldn't want any eliminated from my repertoire. A few words of caution: These special threads are included here with the suggestion that they be used in *sparing* touches. They are best employed to provide highlights and accents or perhaps a spot of texture. I like to see different threads used together in one design, as long as each fits the canvas and suits the eventual purpose of the work.

Persian Wool Yarn

This is a three-strand, loosely twisted thread. Three-strand means that the yarn is made of three strands that are twisted loosely together to form a single length of yarn. Each of the three strands is two-ply. The strands are easily separated to fit different sizes of canvas, hence three-strand yarn is very flexible. Persian wool yarn is available in a broad and dazzling range of shades and colors. Use one strand for Number 18 mesh; two strands for Numbers 14 and 12 mesh; and three strands, or the full thread, for Number 10 mesh.

Combine 7 to 9 strands together for quickpoint, or for Numbers 7, 5, and 3 mesh.

Florentine stitches require *thicker* thread than do other stitches. Use two strands for Number 18 mesh; two strands for Number 16 mesh; three strands for Numbers 14 and 12 mesh.

Tapestry Wool

This is a four-ply yarn, more tightly twisted than Persian wool yarn, that comes in a nice range of colors. It is fine for use with Numbers 10, 12, and 14 mesh canvas but cannot be easily separated for use on finer mesh canvases.

CHECKERBOARD

The large squares are made up of one hundred basketweave stitches worked on Number 12 canvas with two threads of Persian yarn. The small squares are twenty stitches each, all in tones of gray, with white and black. Center the pattern at the start and sprinkle it with plain, opaque white sequins at the finish.

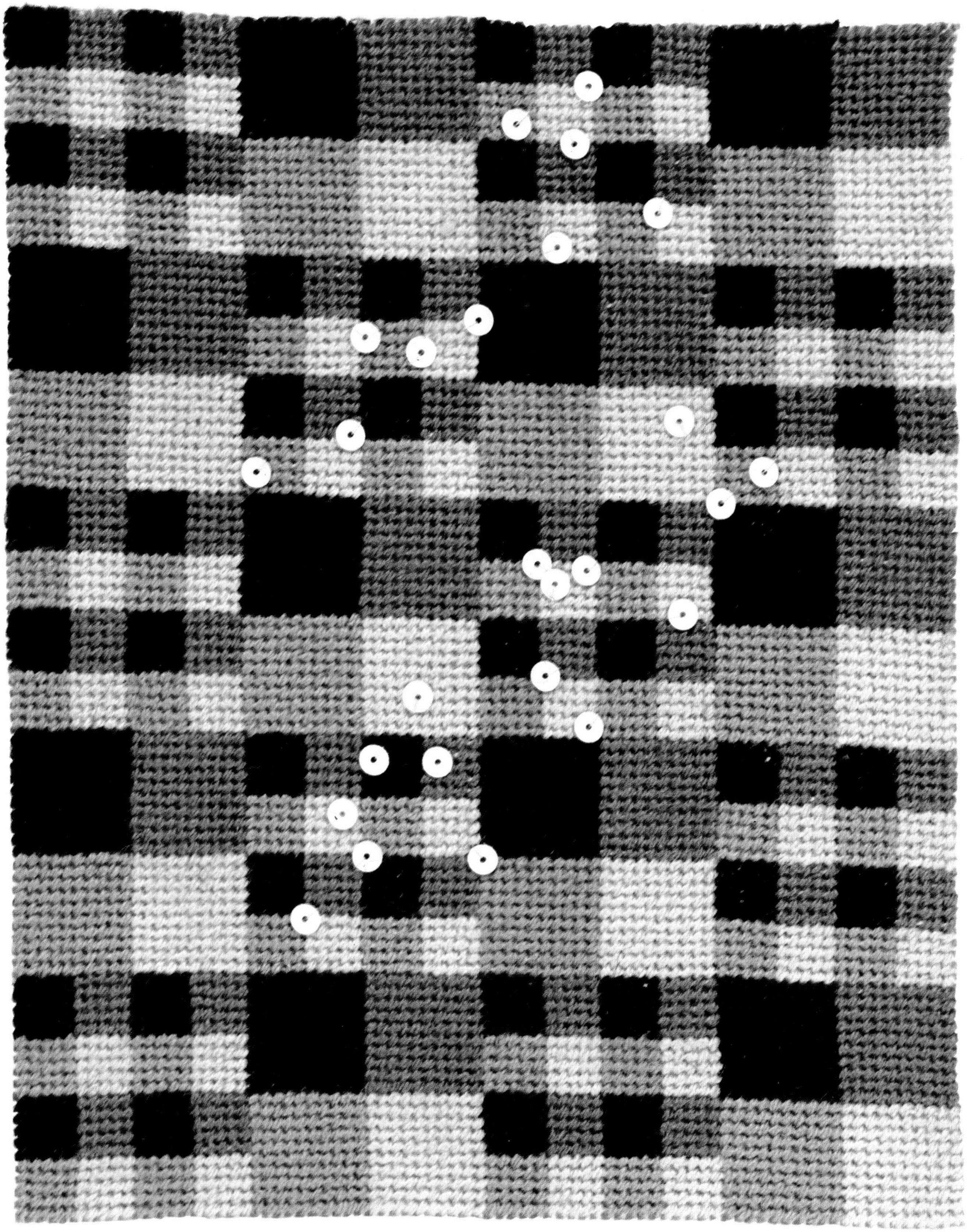

Crewel Wool Yarn

This is a fine two-ply yarn. It is designed to be used as a single thread but can be combined with other single-thread yarns to cover many different sizes ot canvases—I have used as many as five threads together. It is primarily used in needlepoint for Number 18 mesh canvas. It comes in a broad range of lively shades and colors.

Rug Wool

This is a thick, four-ply, rough-textured thread, most often used in making rugs, wall hangings, or other large-scale projects. Rug wool will cover canvas Number 8 mesh and larger; it is useful in quick-point designs for pillows where texture, bold design, and quick results are desired. Because rug wool is thick, it is not a flexible material. It is difficult to combine other yarns with it. I found it cumbersome to handle and a bit gross except for rugs. Also, it is hard to get detail using rug wool.

DMC Stranded Cotton—Mouline Special

This thread resembles silk but is easier to handle and more durable than silk. It adds a touch of elegance to pattern and it contrasts nicely with wool: smooth against rough; lustrous against flat; silky next to woolly. Use the whole strand on Number 16 mesh. Thicken it by doubling or tripling where necessary. Try to keep this yarn untwisted as you stitch because the strands tend to separate when they are worked.

Twilley's Goldfingering Yarn

This is a washable, nontarnishable metallic thread of 80 percent viscose duracol and 20 percent metallic polyester. It is strikingly beautiful in combination with wool and exquisite when used in elegant or formal patterns. Use it as a highlight and as an accent when you want a dressy effect. It comes in marvelous colors—especially the bronze, copper, fuchsia, gold, and silver. Since it is a thin thread, you may have to double it to make it a better cover for the larger mesh canvases, though a heavier variety is now being made that comes in gold and silver only. Keep the threads untwisted. This yarn handles very nicely.

Jaeger Chenille

This yarn is 68 percent viscose and 32 percent cotton. It is a rather thick thread with a nubby velvety texture. It is most successfully used on mesh sizes Number 14, 12, and 10. It makes a fat, beautiful French knot, and it seems to work better for Florentine stitches than it does for the tent stitch. You should explore its possibilities and draw your own conclusions, using it where you think best. However, do use a large needle, perhaps Number 13, when using this yarn. Explore, experiment!

Springer Rayon Embroidery Thread

This is a loosely twisted, fine twelve-ply thread. It is very flexible and can be doubled and redoubled if necessary. The high sheen of this embroidery thread provides a dramatic contrast to wool and makes it a useful and interesting thread for high-lighting and accenting design. It is a bit slippery in the needle, however.

Knox Linen Floss

This rather fine two-ply thread may be tripled for use on canvas. It is hard wearing, and like any other linen thread, it has long fibers and gives a rather flat, smooth effect when worked in the tent stitch or similar stitches.

Knitting Wools

Many people enjoy using these variegated types of yarn for a hit-or-miss design because of their random spots of color. Knitting wools can be worked in combination with Persian and other threads, but they are not quite as durable as yarn designed for needlepoint. They are a bit soft, and will "pill."

Pearl Cotton Thread

This twisted, extremely lustrous thread also provides a nice contrast to wool. Use it in articles that are not destined for hard wear. Number 3 is a useful size for needlepoint, but the threads may have to be doubled in order to cover all but the larger canvases.

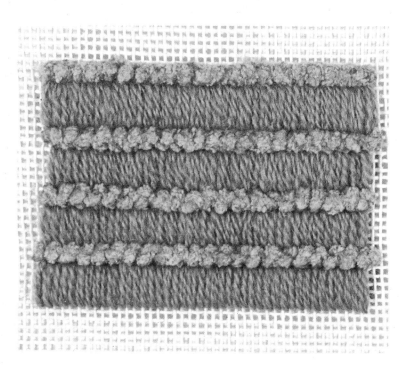

KNOTTED STRIPES

The nubby, velvety texture of chenille shows up strikingly when it is used, as it is here, to make rows of fat French knots between smooth stripes of Gobelin stitches in Persian wool. The knots were worked with one thread of chenille, the Gobelin stitches with three strands of Persian yarn, on Number 14 canvas.

OTHER TOOLS AND EQUIPMENT

Everyone has special tools, materials, or equipment that he likes to work with. Here are some suggestions.

Needles (Tapestry Needles)

These are blunt-tipped steel with long oval eyes. The eye should be wide enough for easy threading, and the thread should pass through the eye smoothly—without fraying, pulling, or snagging. Use the best quality needle you can find—it *does* make a difference. Needles are numbered; the higher the number, the finer the needle: Sizes 17 and 18 are best for Number 10 canvas. Sizes 18, 19, 20, and 22 are best for Number 12, 14, 16, and 18 canvases. Sizes 13, 14, and 15 are best for quick-point stitching with rug yarn on Number 7, 5, and 3 canvases.

Tape Measure and Rulers

These tools are necessary for finding the center of the canvas, drawing margins, cutting canvas, blocking a worked piece into shape, and other operations.

Thimble

This is also really an optional item, but I prefer it to a calloused fingertip.

Masking Tape

One-inch wide tape is most useful for binding the cut edges of the canvas.

Graph Paper

The best type to use is the kind that has the squares divided into blocks of ten by a heavier or dark blue line. Graph paper is indispensable if you want to plan a design on paper before working on the canvas.

Magnifying Glass

A good quality glass is useful in counting the stitches in a pattern, and it will help to detect missing stitches or other mistakes in worked needlepoint.

Needlepoint Frames

In England, frames are widely used to hold the canvas for almost all needlepoint, but they are not as popular in America since the frame restricts the embroiderer, and one of the joys of needlepoint is that you can take your work almost everywhere.

Marking Pens

There are many new color markers and pens on the market; some are advertised as waterproof or color fast. Things are not always what they seem! Even if each pen is marked waterproof and permanent, it should be tested on a swatch of canvas that is then worked and later dipped in water. Color markers and pens have been known to run and to stain a piece of lovely work, rendering it useless.

Scissors

Two pairs are useful: a tiny pair with narrow, pointed blades, and a large pair for cutting canvas and masking tape. A practical and pretty item is a ribbon—weighted at one end, with your scissors tied to the other end—that goes over your shoulders. The scissors are then always available to your stitching hand—and not hidden under the seat cushion or on the floor out of reach.

Pencils

Use hard lead pencils to mark guidelines or to indicate the center of your canvas.

Beads, Sequins, and Jewels

You will notice that several patterns in this book include beads, sequins, jewels, and other embellishments, which add a richly decorative element to needlepoint designs. This idea is not new—the Elizabethans used gold and silver threads, pearls, beads, spangles, and metal wire in their needlework, and the Indians of Madras still include seeds, beans, and tiny mirrors in theirs. Mixing media like this can glorify and individualize a creative idea: A stitch can be underscored by a bugle bead, or a whole flower can grow around a wooden button. Use anything your imagination lights on, if you believe in its creative integrity.

If you wish to add these elements to your designs, do it with discretion, and mostly in purely decorative needlepoint, such as picture or mirror frames, evening bags, wall hangings, or special apparel that does not receive constant wear.

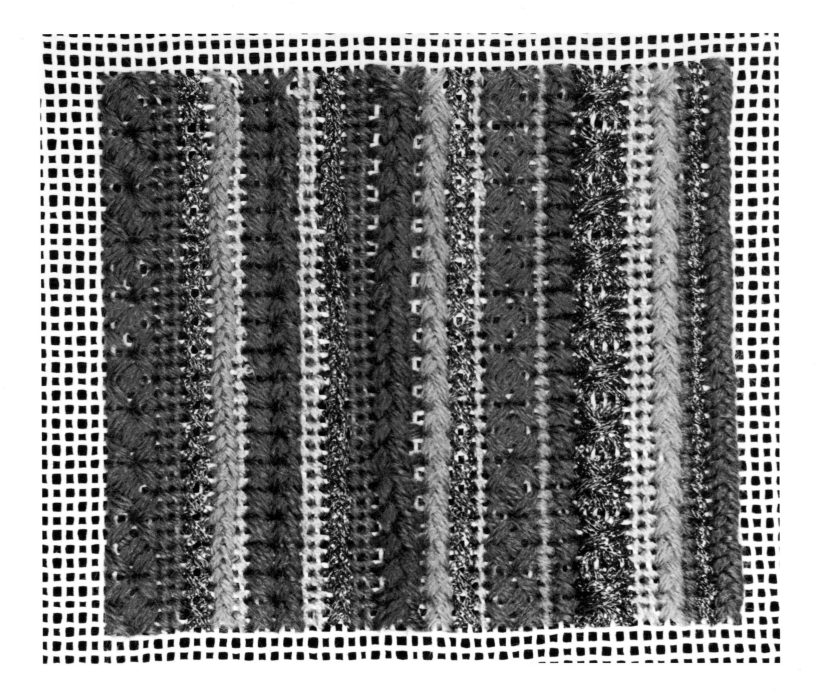

24

4 GETTING STARTED

There are several important decisions to make before you start any needlepoint project. The first one, of course, is to determine the purpose or use for the completed work. The next step is to choose the stitches that will be used and then the threads and colors with which to develop the design. If you are making a rug, you should use wool yarn intended for hard wear; the stitches should also be chosen with this in mind. A wall hanging can be covered with loose, long stitches worked in frivolous and fragile threads. It can be dotted with beads or accented with stones, jewels, sequins, or wooden forms. An eyeglass case requires a small-scale design, which in turn demands a fine canvas. Although any threads will do, if the case is to be carried in a purse and subjected to constant fingering, it should be worked in a durable yarn. Long stitches and fancy threads don't belong on a piano bench used daily by growing children. An evening bolero can be wildly colorful but should be flattering to its wearer in every way—scale, color, and design.

After you've decided on the purpose of the work, the stitches you will use, and the pattern, you are ready to prepare your canvas. Measure out the canvas you will need, and then add 4 inches to each dimension. Always cut your canvas with a seam allowance of 2 inches per side on each of the four sides of the piece; this extra allowance is for subsequent blocking, mounting, and any slight shrinkage from working the stitches. A finished ten-inch pillow starts out as a fourteen-inch pillow overall.

Using one-inch-wide masking tape, bind the edges of the canvas by folding the tape over all four edges. Or machine hem to check raveling. Obviously, selvage edges do not need to be bound.

Keep the selvage edges to the sides of the can-

STRIPE SAMPLER

A sampler explores and records different threads and stitches used in varying combinations. The simple stripe pattern shown here illustrates the interplay of different colors and textures. It was worked on Number 10 canvas with different thicknesses of threads, depending on the stitch or variety of thread used—in this sampler I worked with metallic, wool, and silk threads.

vas and mark the top of the bound or hemmed canvas with the word *Top.* This is a good reference point and it acts as a reminder *not to turn your work sideways*—unless the pattern directs you to. Keeping the word *Top* at the upper part of your work ensures a consistent, even slant to all your stitches. When you do mean to turn your canvas to complete an unfinished half, be sure to turn it upside down, with the word *Top* upside down at the bottom. In this way the top becomes the bottom and vice versa, and the stitches will all be slanted in the same direction.

If you are working your needlepoint patterns from the diagrams in this book, you should read the diagrams by counting threads, not open meshes. That is, count the number of canvas threads or intersections between where the needle comes out and where it goes in. The diagrams of the stitches that are included with each pattern will guide you step by step in your counting.

Each stitch has its own numbered sequence: Odd numbers indicate when the needle is brought "out" of the canvas from the underside to the working surface; even numbers show the needle going back "in" from the surface to the underside.

In the pattern diagrams, shading and color are indicated by two values of gray in addition to white and black. These shadings are simply a guide. You can adopt them and use them just as they are, that is, use the same color every place that black and white or that the same shade of gray appears. Or, make your own choices and use a light color for black and a dark for white. Each diagram and pattern should be used as flexibly as possible. For example: for every black you might use hot pink; for white, a yellow; for dark gray, a kelly green; for light gray, a lettuce green. In this way the pattern is interpreted in a more personal color scheme.

Close-up photographs will back up the diagrams to give you a more complete visual idea of the design pattern and the stitch. Often the photograph is all you will need to work from. Study it and feel free to use a magnifying glass to count stitches or analyze the design. Where the graph shows only the first row or the outline of one complete motif, it will be absolutely necessary to consult the photograph to check the design details and the order of colors or shades.

Unless I have indicated otherwise, all counted needlepoint patterns should be started in the center of the canvas. Draw an even margin around the four sides of the design area using a ruler and margin lines; then measure across and down the canvas to find the vertical thread that is equidistant from the sides and the horizontal thread that is equidistant from the sides. At their intersection, mark the *top* of each of these threads—not between them—with a pencil line, making a small light cross to use as a guideline. Do this marking with a hard lead pencil. The pencil line will not smear and the light pencil mark makes a good guideline. You can also use a pale pink or lemon marker and just make a dot at the center intersection. These colors won't intrude through the threads of your design.

CENTERING THE DESIGN

Unless I have indicated otherwise, always center your designs so that they will end evenly at the margin lines. In this case the center was found by marking the canvas intersections along diagonal lines running from corner to corner; the spot where they crossed was marked with a cross stitch, and the design—four motifs of "Florentine Gems" (see page 83)—grew outward from there.

26

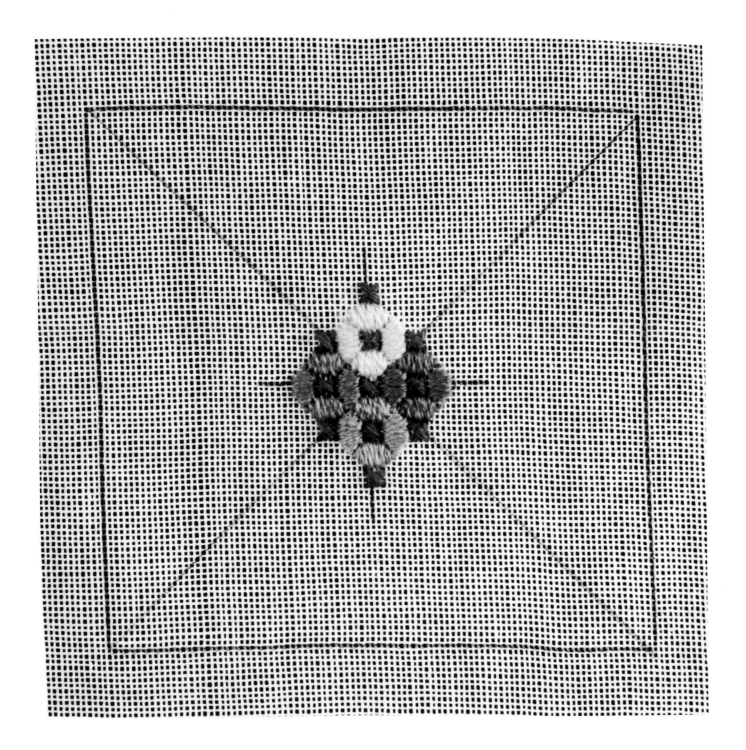

Once the center of your canvas is defined, you are ready to work the first stitch—the center stitch of the design motif—over that mark. The design will grow outward stitch by stitch from the center and should finish evenly at the margins.

Any pattern can be laid out on graph paper, since the vertical and horizontal lines of the graph paper exactly represent the threads of your canvas. When a stitch is a long, straight one, such as a Florentine stitch, count the horizontal lines on the graph over which the stitch will pass.

When you are transcribing a motif from graph paper to canvas, you may want to make small adjustments, or to change a stitch here and there. This is a form of poetic license, which is always entirely acceptable. If the motif is part of a repeating design pattern, the change must of course appear in each of the repeated figures. I seldom use graph paper myself; instead I do my designing by trial and error directly on canvas with needle and thread until I'm satisfied. Find the way that suits you without making it into an academic venture; but remember that the size canvas you choose will affect the design. If the pattern is worked on quickpoint, the overall design will be larger but there will be fewer motifs.

When using a Number 16 mesh canvas, you will get a smaller overall design, and there will be more design motifs in the same number of inches of finished work. So plan accordingly. See the fleur-de-lis worked on three sizes of canvas (see pp. 14–15). There are obviously going to be fewer repeats of the fleur-de-lis on quickpoint than on a Number 14 canvas.

BUYING YARN

It is always difficult to calculate exactly the amount of yarn for a specific project. Be sure to buy more yarn than you need. Dye lots change and exact matching can be a problem. Leftovers are never wasted; they are great for hit-or-miss designs, experiments, spots of interest, and patchwork patterns. The amount of extra yarn varies with every piece of needlework. Beginners waste more yarn than experienced craftsmen do—they make more mistakes and must rip them out—and because they may exert uneven tension it is more difficult to estimate their needs. If you're in doubt simply ask for advice from your needlepoint supplier.

When you're working with dark colors, you may need to use an extra strand of yarn for a thorough coverage of the canvas. Dark colors sometimes fail to cover white canvas; occasionally they run thinner, perhaps due to dye. I compensate by adding one strand.

THE FIRST STITCH

Thread your needle, keeping your working thread about 18 to 20 inches long—shorter when you are working on fine canvas, and longer when working on heavy canvas or doing quickpoint. Bring the needle from the underside of the canvas to the front side, leaving a two-inch tail of thread behind on the underside. While making the first few stitches, manipulate this tail of thread so that it is sewn down securely on the underside of the canvas by the stitches that you make. Eight or ten stitches should lash down the tail end of your thread to secure it firmly. Avoid making knots, as they can create bumps on the topside of the work.

To finish a thread on the underside of the canvas, run the needle and threads in and out of about eight of the already worked stitches. After starting and finishing in this way, it is safe to clip the ends closely. Long ends tangle, and sometimes work up to the topside, snagging new stitches.

If you must pull out a stitch, unthread the needle, and use the blunt tip to lift the errant stitch up, gently pulling the threads through the mesh until the stitch is out. Rethread your needle and carry on. Trying to go back through the canvas to undo or remove a stitch can cause a chaotic tangle. I've tried it; it doesn't work.

Feel free to roll, crush, or fold your canvas for ease of handling and working. Blocking the finished needlepoint will smooth out the kinks.

THE SAMPLER

For learning, practicing, exploring, or experimenting I can think of nothing better than the time-honored sampler or practice piece. Here is where you can truly see, in context, untried color combinations and textural contrasts, and where you can test the maneuverability of fancy threads. Here is also where you begin to get a sense of scale and to grasp the way stitches relate to each other and to other elements of design. Sometimes I draw a circle or a half moon on my canvas and then fill it in with a particular stitch, trying to see how the stitch fits the shape.

Explore on your sampler: use colors you've never used before; use a new stitch or a new thread, a metallic perhaps, with an old familiar stitch. Notice how the same stitch looks when worked in wool, and then in a contrasting, smooth silky thread. It is easy to learn the mechanics of a stitch; exhaust all its possibilities, not on paper, but with thread and canvas.

Today many people make rather formal samplers —squares or borders of different stitches and colors, each square often outlined, for unity, in the same color. I find this approach busy and confusing and less informative for you if at a later time you try to analyze just what you did to achieve an effect. I prefer a spot sampler that emerges with stitch jottings at random intervals on a piece of 12-inch by 12-inch canvas. In a way, these experimental sketches are vignettes of mini-designs, with one inch of space left around each for clarity and perspective. A few rows of blank canvas around each sample pattern will enable you to count the stitches in a motif.

Try changing the scale of a stitch, making it longer, shorter, or higher. Or change its angle. Stitch it in opposing directions—horizontally, diagonally, in a circular way. A Florentine stitch can be worked through the same slot in the canvas twice, achieving a bulky, high-rise, textured surface. Work some stitches unevenly; for example, make a few tent stitches that go over one intersection of canvas threads in the traditional way, then suddenly work some over two intersections. A few short rows of your design leave you a record that will be useful any time. Make notes of any special effects and jottings, and file them away with your sampler. You will learn a lot in a little time, and the urge to be creative will keep you going—try little variations or completely new schemes.

HIT OR MISS SQUARES

Leftover colors worked in quickpoint in the continental stitch make a gay rug. If you use this pattern for a pillow, add three rows of tent stitches in one color around the four sides for seam allowance. The mating of colors is up to you, but it takes about nine strands of Persian yarn to cover the canvas. (One strand of rug yarn.)

The stripe is always interesting, and is an extremely simple pattern to plan and work on a sampler. A series of lines laid out vertically, horizontally, or diagonally, stripes can be spaced in any way you choose: they can be zigzag, wavy, or straight bands. You may want to alternate wide and narrow stripes in a symmetrical order, or bands in high and low relief. You might even arrange the stripes in an unpredictable, random way: thick, thin, thin, thick, and so on. A striped design does not have to be started in the center of the canvas—an extra bonus for a sampler that is devoted to experimental ideas—but it is helpful to work from the top down. To vary the design, and avoid a monotonous repetition, use a variety of stitches for the assortment of stripes.

As for color, you might try a monotone scheme, concentrating on four or five shades of the same color. They can be either closely graded or dramatically random shades.

Texture results when raised stitches are worked in combination with flat ones, as when you combine the tent, rice, Smyrna, and Gobelin stitches. The tent stitch is flat; the rice stitch is quite rough; the Smyrna is raised and square in shape; and the Gobelin is smooth and flat. To further underscore the texture, use different threads: wool balanced with a pearl cotton and rayon, or flat with shiny. (A word of caution—if you use as many as three or four different stitches, limit the colors and shades you work with. An effective design could be worked in one shade only.) You will begin to discover the pleasures of pattern when you behold your first finished handiwork. Although it is a beginning effort, it is by no means conventional or mundane. And it is completely yours—in color, texture, concept, and execution.

You might enjoy having your first sampler made into a pillow for your sofa or bed. A pillow is an easy first project because it doesn't have to conform to a given shape. A miscalculation on a chair seat could be a disaster, but a pillow—even if it is smaller than you planned—can still be mounted and used. This first pattern-design experience should give you enough confidence to send you rushing to the nearest source of supplies and materials with an urge to express your next artistic idea through stitchery. Be patient and persistent. Try a few more experiments; you'll find your self-confidence, your imagination, and your skill growing at the same time.

The sampler was the earliest pattern book in the history of needlework. Cherished stitches and designs were recorded on a strip of linen and exchanged between friends. They were bequeathed as a treasured legacy. If you want to make your own sampler book, here is a suggestion: Make several samplers a bit smaller than the size of a standard looseleaf page. They can be kept in plastic photograph covers and stored in a looseleaf binder, or they can be filed in manila folders for easy storage and handy reference. A few of these samplers will provide you with stitches, motifs, and patterns for years.

One last note: don't throw anything away. Today's goof may be the beginning of tomorrow's coup. Styles and tastes change—yours will, too. You learn as much from your mistakes as from your successes. Many accidents are happy ones. Sometimes you feel free and frivolous, so you break all the rules with a piece of work that isn't too serious. Not only is it fun, but you can learn more about being free and inventive from that work than you can from the text of a whole book. And a record of your stitchery is a delightful personal diary.

PART II

5 THE STITCHES

Stitches are ways of using thread decoratively; they and the techniques for working them have evolved in every country in every part of the world over the centuries. Stitches are sometimes named for the place of their origin, such as the Hungarian and Florentine stitches. Others just happen to have several names. The rice stitch, for example, is also called the crossed corners stitch and the William and Mary stitch.

Learning to execute a few basic stitches is fairly simple, but it takes practice and ingenuity to use them creatively.

Stitches are basically short or long and slanted, horizontal or vertical. The way they are used and combined produces most of the stitches we know— variations on one stitch can result in another stitch. A tent stitch, elongated, becomes a tilted Gobelin. Some stitches are crossed, some looped, and others knotted.

Short, slanted stitches like the tent stitch require a finer thread than long, straight stitches like the Florentine stitch. Each stitch has a distinct contour or shape that is changed by the use of thick or thin threads, the choice of color, and the scale or size. Each stitch has a personality that can be emphasized or altered by your vision and way of using the stitch, by your changing its angle or direction. Stitches can be single, like the tent and Florentine stitch, or multiple, like the leaf and the Smyrna stitch—there are times when a multiple of as many as eleven small stitches is considered as one single stitch.

HOW THIS BOOK IS TO BE USED

The array of patterns that follow are for all who respond to the luxuriantly tactile appeal of textiles in the form of fiber, stitch, and needle. They invite personal, inventive involvement in all the ways of using materials and tools in the expression of unique and fresh ideas.

The patterns in this book are all variations of themes based on just sixteen stitches. Many marvelous stitches have been left out, but those I use lend themselves to the patterns in a special way. Any other group of stitches would have sparked different but not less fascinating designs. You will discover that the stitches and their patterns are not always grouped or placed together. The tent stitch and its patterns, for example, appear together in one chapter but occasionally the tent stitch may be used in a pattern with another stitch and be classified in the chapter with that stitch. In some cases, a pattern will appear according to color or texture instead of stitch, in order to illustrate a specific effect or point.

This is not strictly a beginner's book, nor is it a glossary, written to define every known embroidery stitch. I have tried to lead the way to innovative thinking and tasteful improvisation with a select number of stitches.

The focus here is on *your* personal pattern discoveries and the realization of your potential as a designer with wider and deeper vision.

LIST OF STITCHES

Short Stitches or
The Tent Stitch

The Continental Stitch
The Basketweave Stitch

Long Stitches

The Gobelin Stitch
The Hungarian Stitch
The Florentine Stitch

Crossed Stitches

The Cross-Stitch
The Smyrna or Double Cross-Stitch
The Rice Stitch

Special Effects Stitches

The Rhodes Stitch
The Leaf Stitch
The Diamond Eyelet Stitch
The Four-sided Stitch
The French Knot

TENT STITCH SAMPLER

Six different tent stitch patterns and six different border designs are combined in a sampler that is not only a useful reference but is so integrated and lovely that it could serve as a finished textile. Each design is easily visualized and counted from the photograph to the canvas.

6 SHORT STITCHES

THE TENT STITCH

The tent stitch is the basic needlepoint stitch. It is usually worked over a single intersection of horizontal and vertical canvas threads, from lower left to upper right. This small, maneuverable stitch should always slant in the same direction, whether you work it in horizontal, vertical, or diagonal rows. Whatever the working sequence, the completed needlepoint will look the same topside. The tent stitch is wonderfully helpful for filling in the gaps between larger stitches or motifs because of its tiny size and its maneuverability.

PINE TREES

Work the trees and connecting lines of the pattern in tent stitch first, placing one motif in the center of the canvas. The background is then stitched in the basketweave stitch. This pattern was worked in red and green for a Christmas stocking. (It can also be appropriately tinseled with small glittering silver sequins. You need not be practical here.) It can be varied by shading the trees from the top down and changing the colors altogether. A Number 12 canvas was used with two strands of Persian yarn. Refer to the photograph as you work.

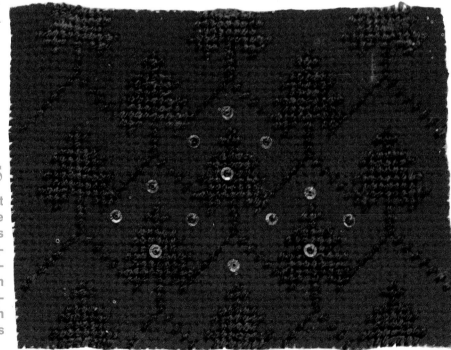

DIAMONDS AND TRIANGLES

The zigzag line is the foundation of this colorful pattern. Starting in the center of the canvas, work the small square of nine tent stitches in the diamond shapes, returning to divide them into four different color triangles separated by a white vertical and horizontal line. Use three strands (the full thread) of Persian wool yarn to cover the Number 10 canvas. I decorated the center of each diamond with a solid white sequin, stitched with fine, white sewing silk and a bead needle. (Any needle that slides through the hole in the sequin will do.)

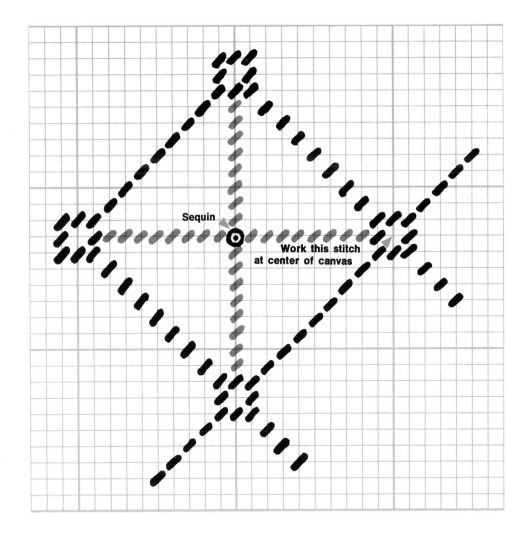

THE CONTINENTAL STITCH

When the tent stitch is worked in horizontal rows from right to left, or in vertical rows from top to bottom, It Is called the contInental stItch. All the stitches should slant in the same direction. When a row is completed, turn the canvas upside down and work back along the row. Each stitch in the second row should be slanting in the same direction as those in the first—from lower left to upper right.

The continental stitch is used to fill in details in a small area, to outline design forms, and to make narrow, straight lines. It can also be used for the background of a design, but it does tend to pull the canvas out of shape, and even though blocking is a great help in reshaping a finished piece, it may not completely straighten a badly out-of-kilter canvas.

40

CONTINENTAL CIRCLES

A perfect example of the use of the continental stitch is this outline of a circle motif that will be filled in later with the basketweave stitch. When the outline of four circles is complete, a small diamond shape emerges. Fill it in with a decorative thread of your own choice.

FRENCH RIBBON

One picture really is worth a thousand words, and this one is no exception. Working from the picture, count the stitches in the vertical and horizontal bands of multicolor ribbon. Much of this pattern will be worked in the continental stitch which will pull the canvas out of shape. Keep your stitching tension easy to counteract this problem. Where there are two rows of a color, you can use the basketweave stitch—in fact, I advise it. Three strands of Persian yarn are used on the Number 10 canvas.

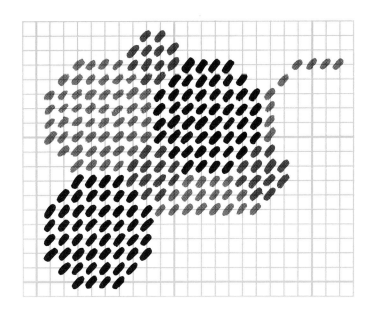

HOT PINK CIRCLES

Note how the colors—hot pink, magenta, and pink metallic in the worked pattern correspond to the tones in the diagram. The lines of the graph symbolize canvas threads, the white squares the meshes. To diagram or graph a pattern yourself, draw a stitch from the center of one white square to the center of another. To read a graph, count the lines or intersections of lines from where the needle comes out to where the needle goes in. This pattern is worked in Persian yarn and pink metallic thread, with an optional trimming of three diagonal satin stitches in D.M.C. stranded cotton. The trimming adds an extra design dimension, but the design holds up beautifully without it. Work the trimming over the already stitched needlepoint. Use two strands of wool and metallic thread and the whole strand of the cotton for proper coverage of the Number 12 canvas.

THE BASKETWEAVE STITCH

The basketweave and the bias tent stitch are names for the tent stitch when it is worked in diagonal rows alternately up and down without turning the canvas. It hardly distorts the canvas or pulls It out of shape. If this stitch is worked with an easy, relaxed tension, it may not even require blocking. Since the work doesn't need to be turned at the end of every row, it can be stitched in an uninterrupted rhythm, making it fast and pleasant going.

The basketweave is worked here as a growing right-angle triangle with a single tent stitch at its apex. Begin at the upper right-hand corner and make a tent stitch; work the second stitch on the same horizontal line and to the left of the one just completed. You now have two stitches side by side. The third stitch is worked directly under the first stitch—a tiny triangle has begun. To start the next diagonal row, work another stitch exactly under the last stitch, and as you complete it, hold the needle horizontally, sliding it under two vertical threads of canvas to bring it out in position to continue up the row. When you reach the top of your diagonal row, turn the needle to a vertical position, pass it under two horizontal threads, and continue *down* the row as your triangle grows larger. Each row dovetails neatly with the one preceding it, forming a handsome and sturdy basketweave on the underside of your work. Just remember to hold your needle *vertically* on "down" rows and *horizontally* on "up" rows. Never stitch two rows in the same direction because a ridge will develop in the surface of your work.

If you are interrupted while working up or down a row, station your needle midrow in position for the

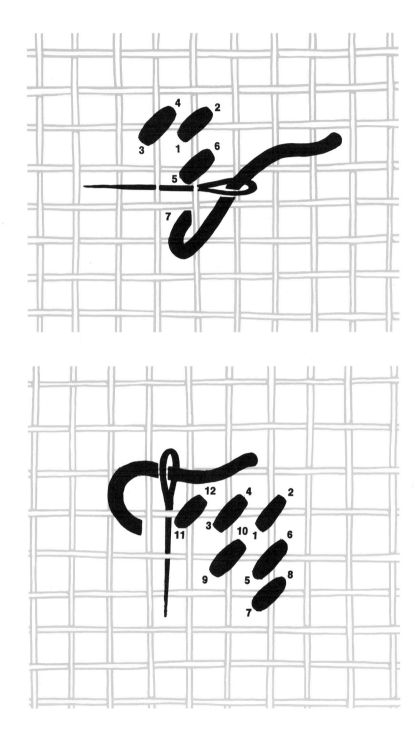

44

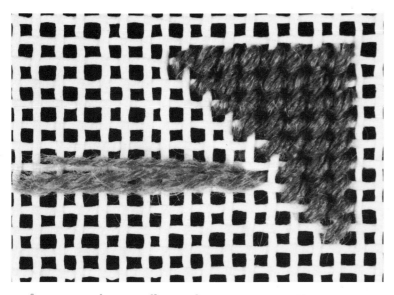

next stitch. This is a sure way of keeping the row sequence straight.

The "Continental Circles" pattern (page 41) is an attractive design using both continental and basketweave stitches that even a novice can work. Be sure to center the first motif of the pattern. Work the outlines for all the circles first with continental stitches, then fill them in with basketweave stitches.

As you work *up* a diagonal row, your needle and thread should slide under the canvas in a *horizontal* direction, from right to left . . .

. . . and as you work *down* the next diagonal row, your needle and thread should slide under the canvas in a *vertical* direction; from the top of the canvas toward you.

GEOMETRIC LEAVES

Mark the exact center of the canvas and work the top- or bottommost stitch of *one leaf,* continuing the outline until it is finished. Next, work the stitches of the veins. Last, work the background color in the basketweave stitch. Put in the second, third, and fourth leaf in the same way, noting that all four leaves meet at the center of the canvas, sharing one stitch. It is easier to keep track of this pattern if you complete each leaf before starting the next. Watch the alternation of the colors, and feel free, of course, to substitute your own. The design is shown on Number 14 canvas with two canvas threads.

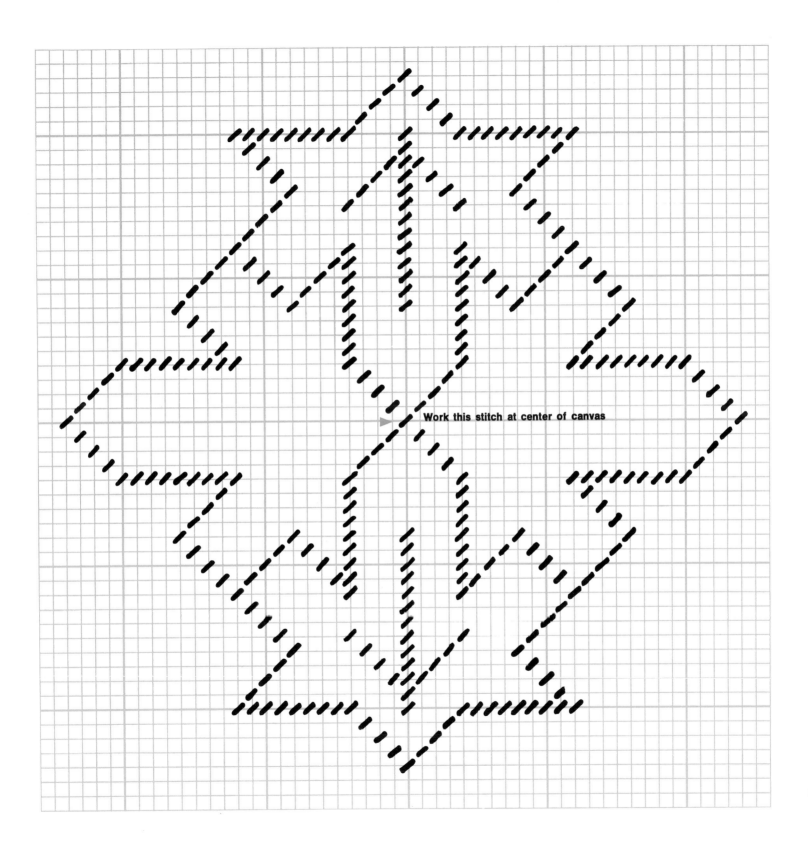

Work this stitch at center of canvas

47

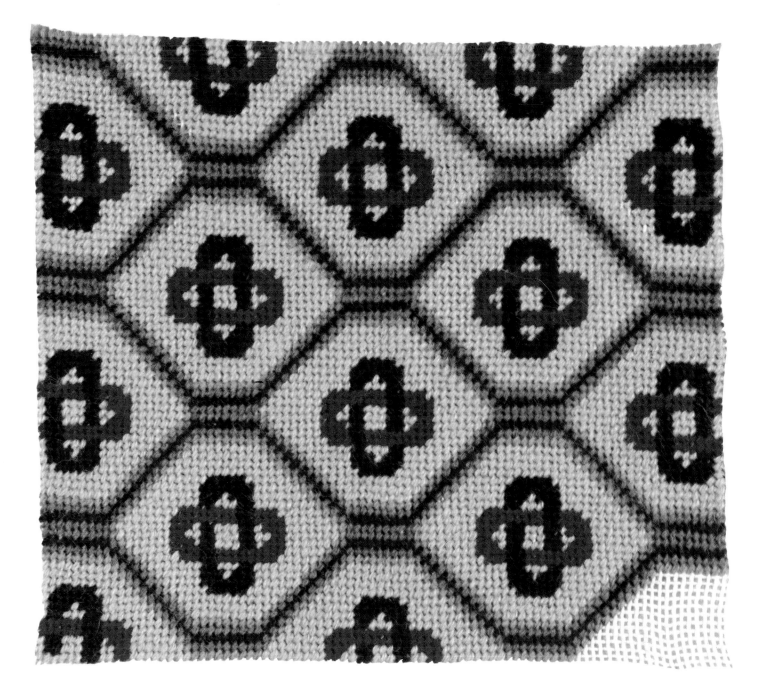

LACED LINKS

Using a dark color, stitch in the entire octagon framework. Fill in with a lighter shade and within that, an even lighter shade. There are now three graduated shades of a color in the pattern. The reversed links, based on a mid-seventeenth century sampler, are worked in the center of the octagon in two colors. Last of all, with an off-white shade, basketweave stitch the background. Two strands of Persian yarn are needed to cover the Number 12 canvas.

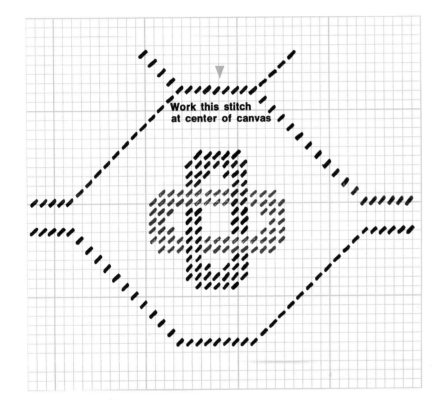

Work this stitch at center of canvas

SILVER-THREADED BASKETWEAVE PATTERN

Worked in tent stitch on Number 12 canvas, this pattern is simple to follow from the photograph. When the entire design is worked, weave the silver thread in and out along the edges of the vertical and horizontal bands of color. I have shown you a "before and after" because the change is so startling and intriguing. The silver thread can be substituted with silk, rayon, cotton, or colored metallic. This is an excellent pattern for slippers, evening bag, or vest and cummerbund but should be worked on a finer canvas (Numbers 16 and/or 14).

50

BUTTERFLIES AND OCTAGONS

Center one complete pattern motif and work outward until the entire octagon framework is finished. Counting carefully, switch the butterflies as the graph indicates, within the octagons. The background, done in basketweave stitch, is worked last. The head of each butterfly is stitched with a small, royal blue, iridescent bead. Two strands of yarn were used on Number 12 canvas.

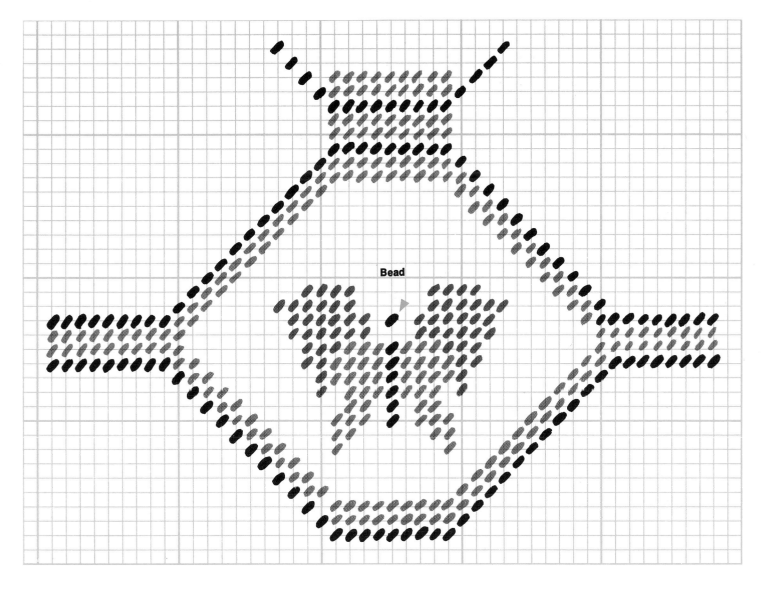

Bead

HONEYCOMB AND BEE

Start the honeycomb pattern in the center of the canvas, but work only one pattern outline as a reference point. Moving away from this point, work the bee, counting it row by row. When it is finished, return to the honeycomb and continue it over your canvas. Fill in with the basketweave stitch when you are satisfied that everything is correct. Any graphed motif can be modified or varied either to suit your taste, the limitations of the canvas, or the dictates of the design. I made a slight change in the antenna of my bee so that it wouldn't get lost in the framework of the honeycomb. Two strands of Persian yarn were used on Number 12 canvas.

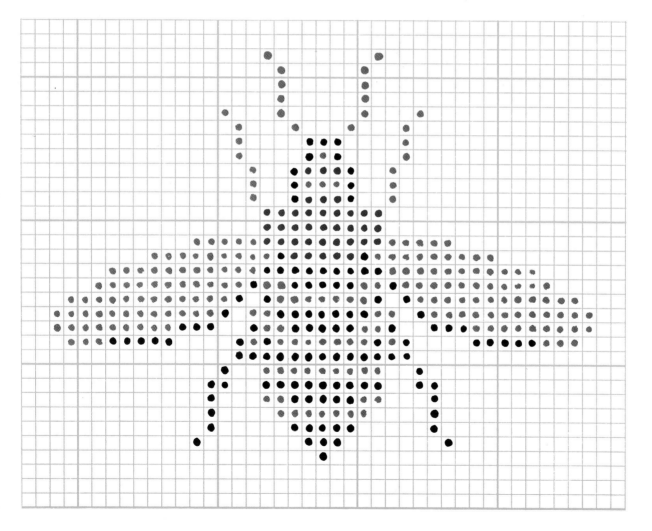

53

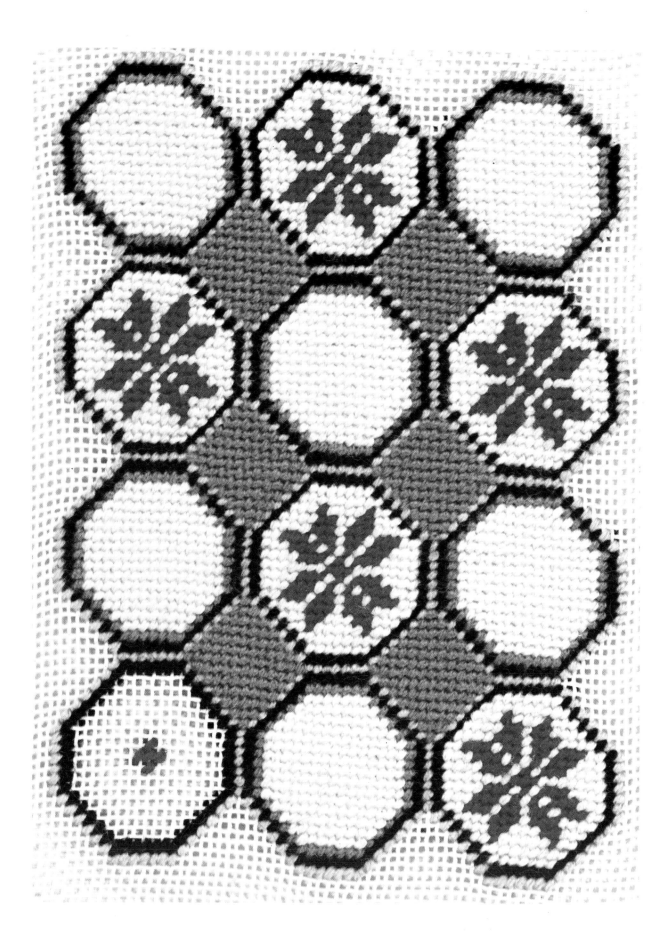

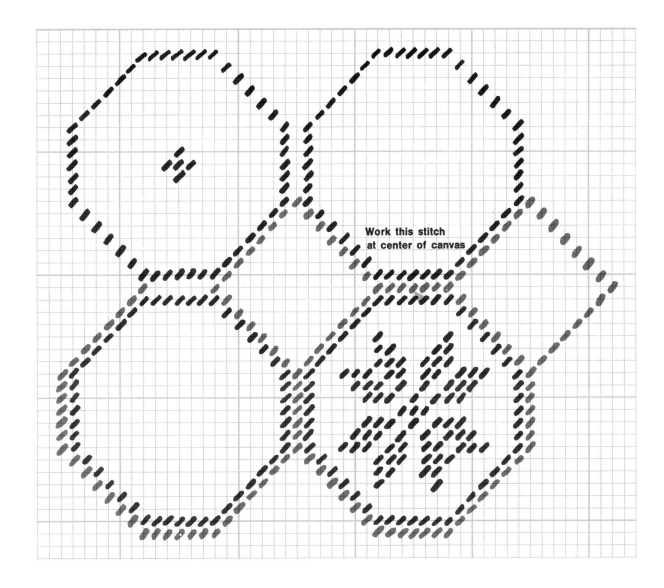

Work this stitch
at center of canvas

OCTAGON FLOWER

Center one octagon and outline the rest of the pattern on
the canvas. Once again, single row outlines are worked in
the continental stitch as are small motifs. The flower must
be stitched in the exact center of an octagon. Note the five
stitches of the unfinished flower in the photograph, they con-
stitute the centermost part of the flower motif positioned in
the center of the octagon. The background is filled in with
the basketweave stitch. This design was worked on Number
10 canvas with three strands of Persian yarn. This framework was used for "Honeycomb and Bee" (see page 52)
and is a very adaptable design motif for any number of
projects.

55

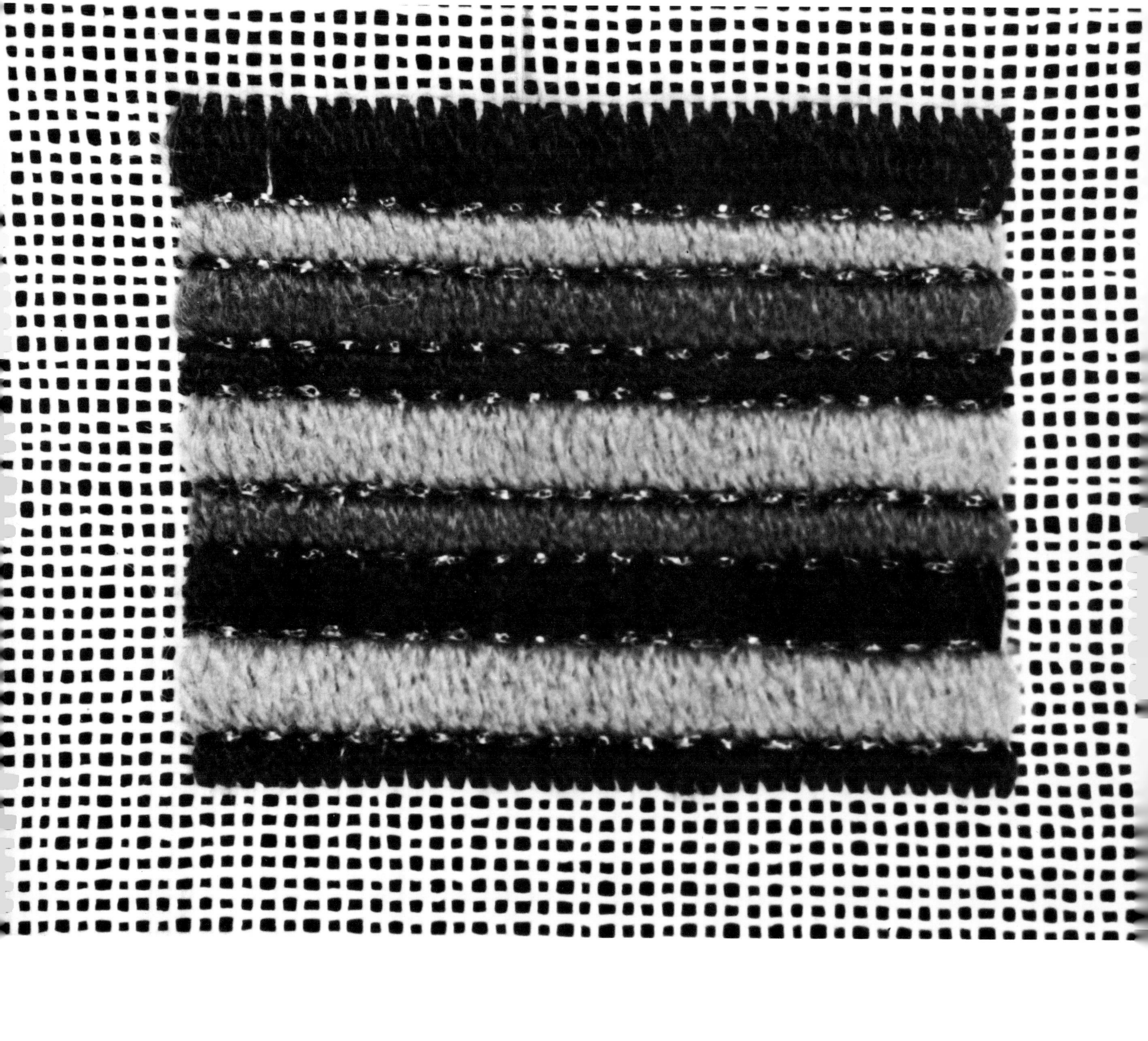

7 LONG STITCHES

THE GOBELIN STITCH

The Gobelin stitch is a very old, upright stitch, identical to the satin stitch in embroidery. It can be worked across a row from left to right or from right to left. The number of horizontal canvas threads over which this vertical stitch is worked may vary from row to row, but within a row the stitch length must be even.

Because the Gobelin is an upright stitch it will pull your canvas much less than a slanting stitch would. It is smoothly textured, can be worked quickly, and covers the canvas rapidly. But this stitch takes a thicker yarn, usually a strand more than you use for a slanting stitch. Keep in mind that you always need a balance between yarn and canvas. When your stitches are longer, you need thicker yarn to cover the canvas. As you work this stitch, keep your yarn flat and untwisted. The tension or pull of the stitch should be kept relaxed to achieve a nice puffed out or quilted surface.

A combination of wide and narrow Gobelin stripes can result in a simple but handsome design. When you want a wider stripe, lengthen the stitches for a row. When you want a narrow stripe, shorten the stitches for a row.

The photograph of Gobelin stripes (on facing page) shows you a distinctive pattern of sophisticated colors. Here mocha, chocolate, and cinnamon stripes are accented with copper metallic thread that was backstitched between each stripe.

In this pattern the backstitch goes over two threads of canvas horizontally. But the backstitch can be worked over any number of vertical or horizontal canvas threads for highlight, accent, or to fill in where the canvas shows.

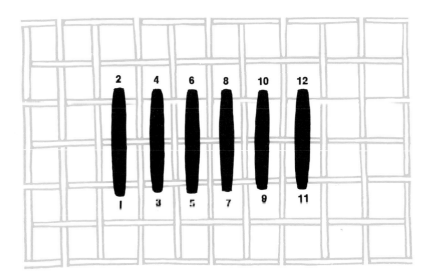

FLOWERETTES

French knots make a charming flower design on a ground of Gobelin stitches worked in different directions. On quick-point, work six strands of Persian yarn over three double canvas threads, turning the canvas as each section of three stitches is finished. Four large French knots (use six strands of Persian yarn) fill the centers. In the top three rows, I used red glass beads as a garnish. In the bottom three rows, a small French knot in chenille thread goes over the top of the bigger ones, giving you two options. The squares in the pattern are worked in the basketweave stitch in a different color.

There are twelve stitches in each flowerette, three to a side. Center the pattern on your canvas.

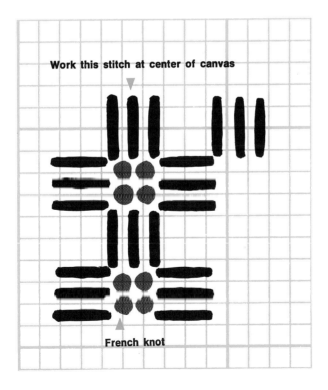

Work this stitch at center of canvas

French knot

THE HUNGARIAN STITCH

The Hungarian stitch forms a diamond pattern based on three upright or vertical stitches. The first stitch is worked vertically over two horizontal threads, the second over four horizontal threads, and the third over two again. Skip one mesh, and repeat the pattern. Continue in this way across the row. The second row will begin with one short stitch over two horizontal threads, followed by one skipped mesh and the pattern of three upright stitches, and so on. As you work more rows, notice how the long stitches of one row fit into the skipped meshes of the row above. Short stitches line up under short stitches and long ones are under long ones—all the way down the canvas.

A bit of distinction can be given the pattern by alternating colors and textures from row to row. Note the textural contrast here between the fuzzy wool and velvety chenille yarn.

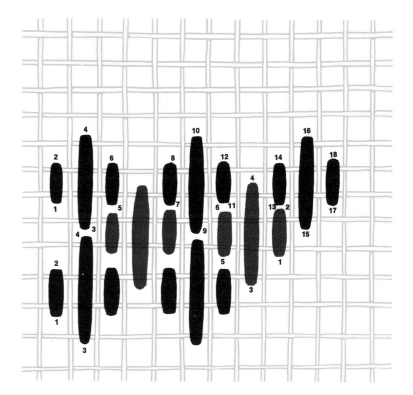

Pillow worked in *Flowers and Squares* pattern. Color changes bring amazing changes in the same pattern. *(Worked by Mrs. James Levi.)*

Pillow worked in *Flowers and Squares, variation number 1* in muted golds and darkly brilliant bittersweets, six shades of each.

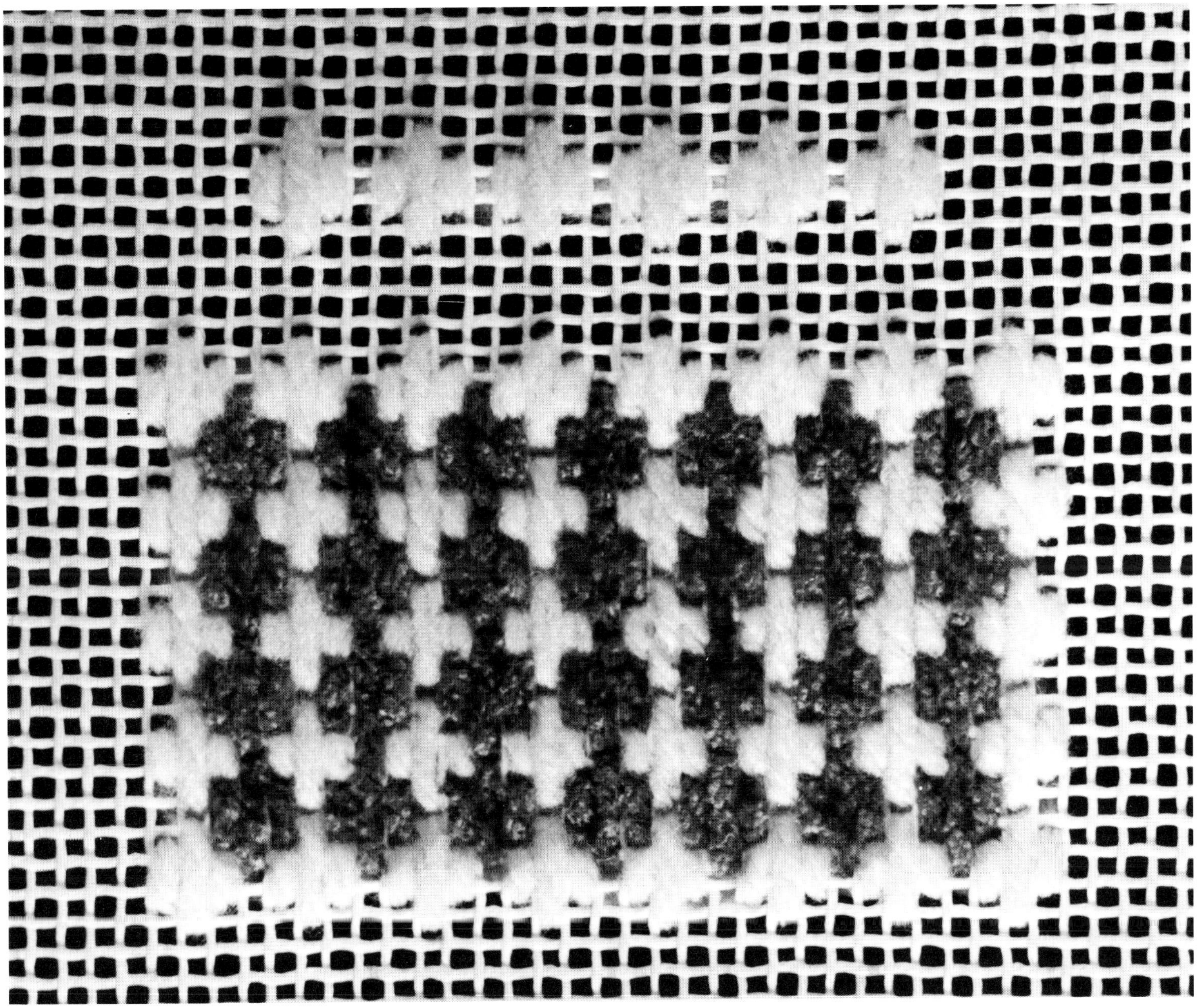

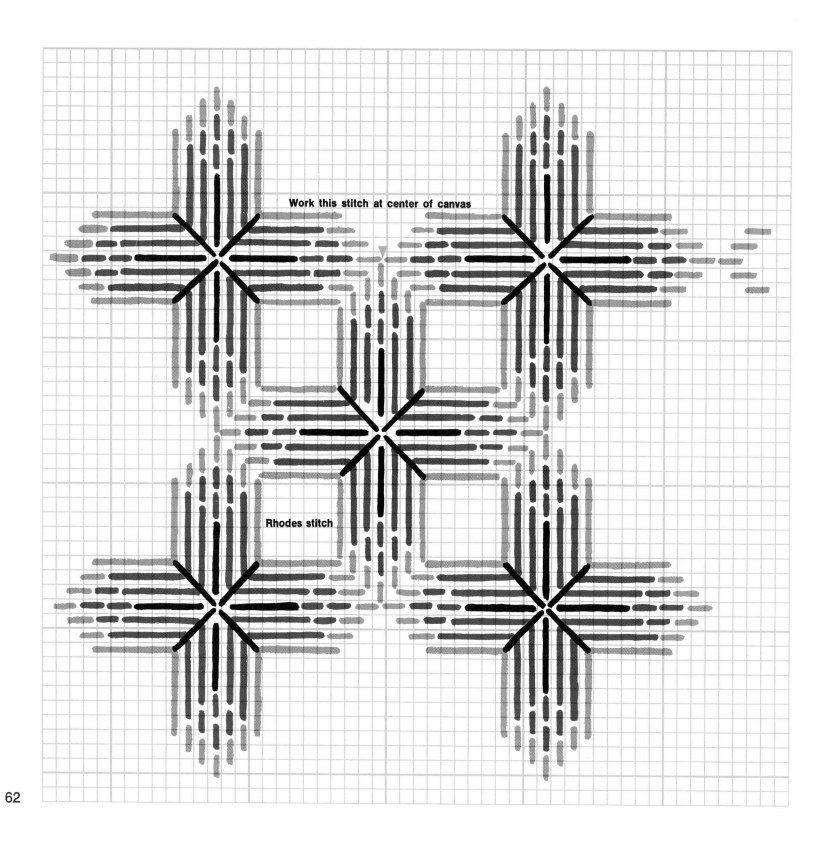

Work this stitch at center of canvas

Rhodes stitch

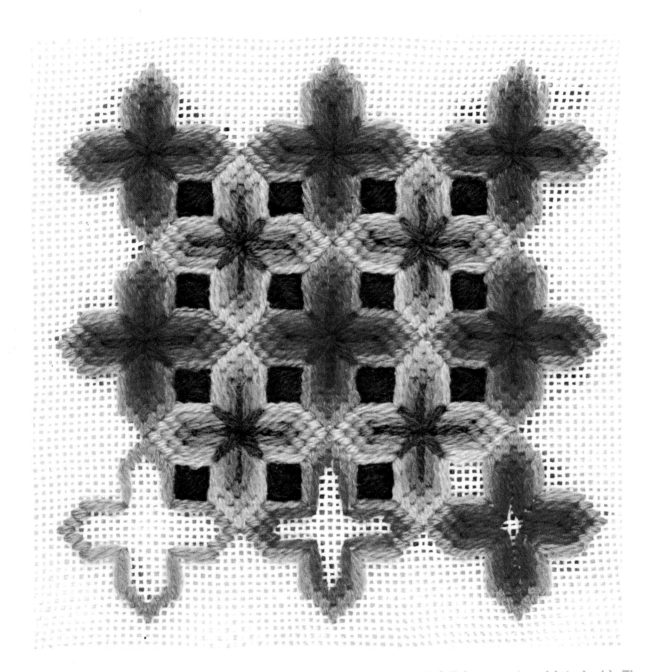

FLOWERS AND SQUARES

This rather complicated pattern is a combination of long and short stitches that are worked in different directions in the same design. There are four shades each of the two colors used, with a third color as the square. The lightest shade is used on the outer edge and the darkest in the center, giving off a nice glow. The flowers are arranged in rows of color both vertically and horizontally, their points sharing the same mesh (all four meet and interlock). Three flowers are shown here in various stages of development as a guide. I like to fill each one completely before outlining the next. The squares emerge when two flowers are completed. Begin this pattern by working the top stitch of a flower over the exact center of your canvas. Four diagonal satin stitches radiate from the centers of all the flowers. Three strands of Persian yarn were used to cover Number 12 canvas.

FLOWERS AND SQUARES
Variation Number One

This variation's wider flower results from the addition of short stitches. Instead of shading, I used a group of unrelated colors in one flower and juxtaposed them in the other. Bronze metallic thread provides the highlight and fills the squares. The centers of the flowers are filled with a cross-stitch. This pattern was worked on Number 16 canvas with two strands of Persian yarn.

Work this cross-stitch in center of canvas

64

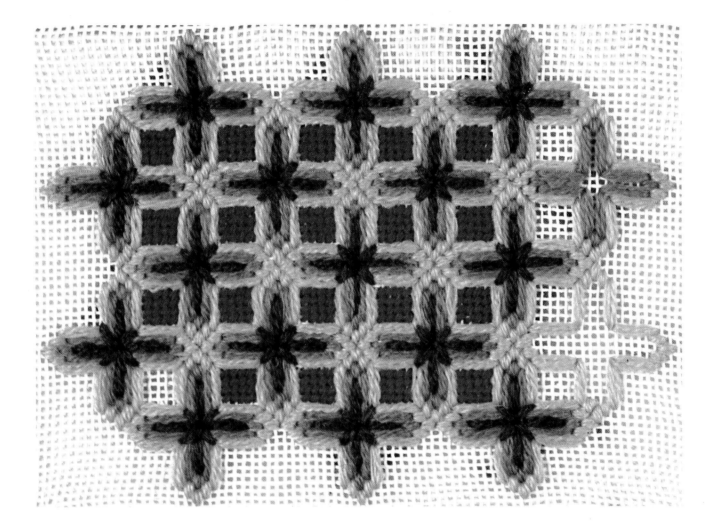

FLOWERS AND SQUARES
Variation Number Two

Three short stitches followed by two long ones combine in this variation of the master Flowers and Squares pattern. The basketweave stitch in one color fills the squares in this version and three shades of another color repeat all over. Four diagonal satin stitches are worked in the center of the flowers in the darkest green. Three strands of Persian yarn are used on Number 12 canvas.

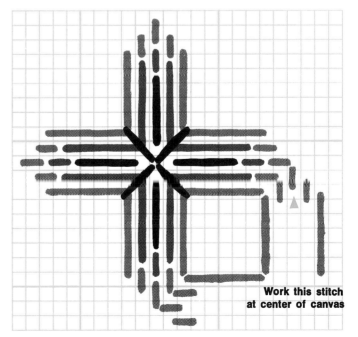

Work this stitch at center of canvas

65

FLOWERS, SQUARES, AND DIAMONDS

The dark brown diamond outline is centered and worked first. Next, work one full flower in the exact center of a diamond. Fill inside it with beige, rust, and white yarn, then repeat the flowers as far as the boundaries of the diamond. What you have here is eight sections of flowers, four squares, and one complete flower. Three diamonds were left in different stages of progress to make the pattern clear. It is worked on Number 16 canvas with two threads of Persian yarn.

This is an advanced pattern and a very elegant one.

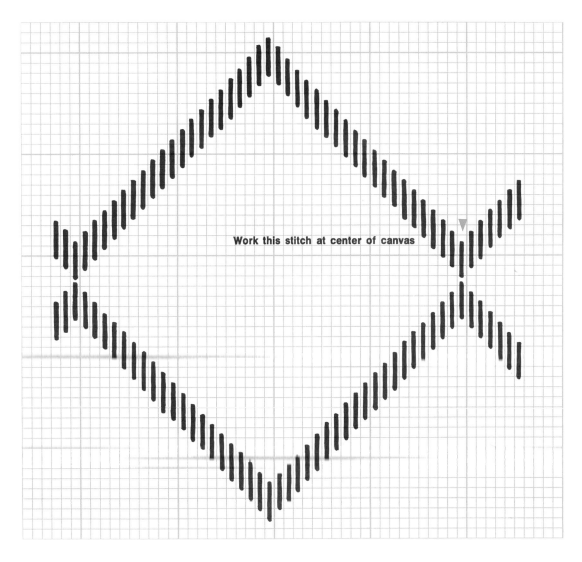

Work this stitch at center of canvas

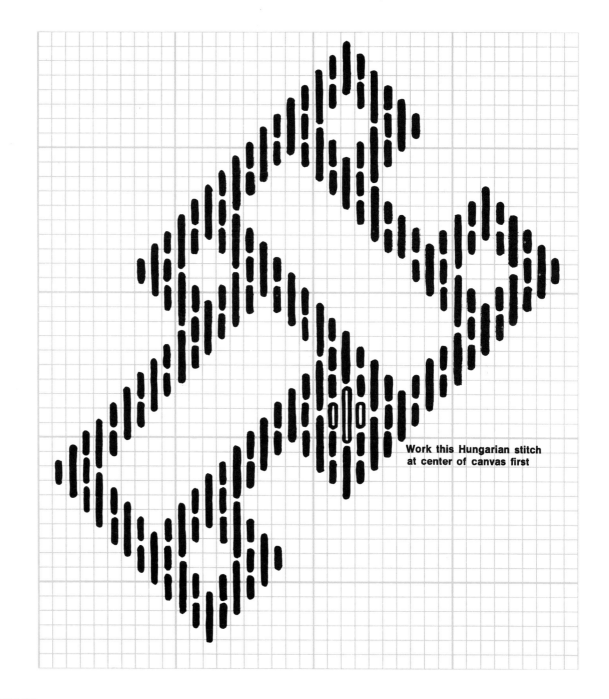

Work this Hungarian stitch
at center of canvas first

HUNGARIAN BASKETRY

All the rectangles of the basketry pattern have a square at each end filled with one unit of Hungarian stitches (three upright stitches). Start by working the three upright stitches in the center of your canvas. Working out from there, complete the outline of a whole rectangle and squares; in order to keep the pattern straight. Include the colors that fill the inside as you go. It is a bit tricky to keep track of the progression but very well worth the effort. Check back often to both the graph and the photograph as you stitch. I used chenille yarn to fill the squares for textural interest and contrast. Two strands of Persian yarn are needed for the Number 12 canvas. Note the alternation of colors in the rectangles.

69

THE FLORENTINE STITCH

The Florentine stitch is an upright stitch based on the Gobelin stitch, but unlike the Gobelin, the Florentine is not arranged in straight rows. Florentine stitches are worked in groups or blocks that move up and down the canvas in rows of rounded arcs, peaks, and valleys. The Florentine stitch can be worked over anything from two to ten horizontal canvas threads, and it is a joy to play with.

The first row of most Florentine patterns should be started in the center of the canvas and worked left to the side margin. Returning to the center, work from there to the right side margin. This completes a whole row from margin to margin. The first row acts as a guideline for the entire design.

To work the next row, begin at the right margin directly under your first row. Follow each stitch exactly as you work across the row so that the second row of stitches dovetails exactly with the first. If the stitch in row 1 covers four horizontal threads of canvas, the stitch below it in row 2 need not do the same; but if the stitch in row 1 *steps down* two horizontal threads from the one next to it, the stitch in row 2 must follow it exactly.

When you have worked across to the left side of the canvas, drop down to row 3 and work back to the right side. Keep working the rows back and forth across the canvas. You will see as you work that each row interlocks with the preceding one. Row follows row downward across the width of the canvas.

When your zigzag rows reach the bottom of the canvas, the valleys will touch the margin but the peaks will not. Just turn the canvas upside down and fill in the gaps between. As a guide, follow the

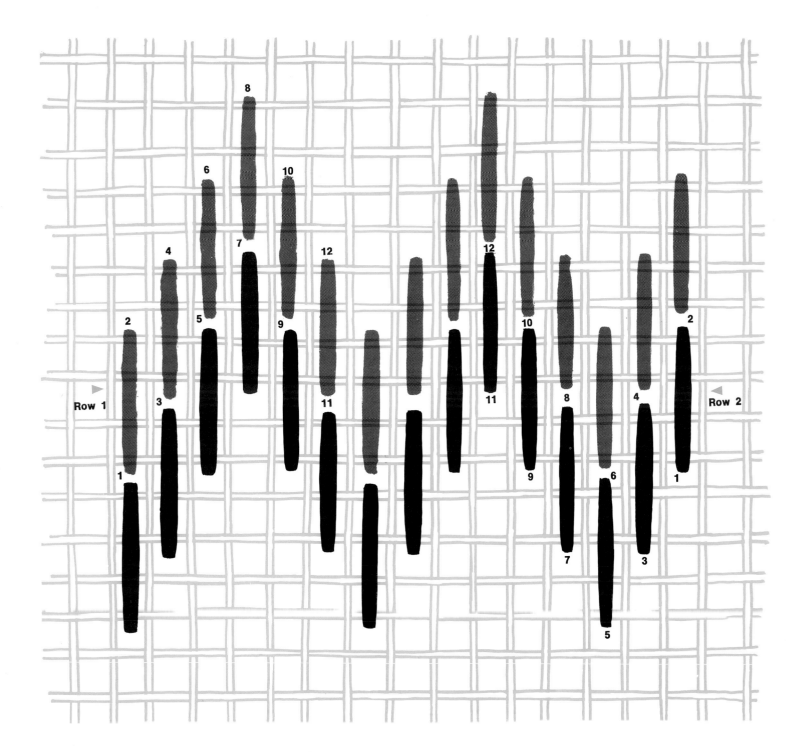

pattern of the other rows but make sure none of the stitches go beyond the margin line.

The Florentine stitch covers a large area very quickly and can produce a satin-smooth surface. Numbers 18, 16, 14, and 12 canvases are the most suitable sizes for Florentine work.

The Florentine stitch can be worked over four horizontal threads and back over two and then again over four threads, stepping two higher or two lower than the stitch just worked. This zigzag line is the most basic pattern of Florentine embroidery —but just one of the infinite potentials of this versatile stitch.

You can arrange your vertical stitches so that each stitch is two threads higher than the preceding one. When your stitches have marched diagonally up to a peak, work down the other side, repeating the same number of stitches in reverse order.

You can alternate groups of stitches across the width of the canvas. The slightest variation invents new patterns. By changing the length of the stitch, the length of the step, and the number of stitches in the group, you will discover new angles and fascinating geometric forms from serrated peaks to rounded arches.

You can begin your experiment on a sampler using this upright stitch in different ways. Work it in even rows, then expand it, working out combinations of short stitches with long ones. Try whatever comes to mind and you are bound to have some pleasant surprises as you learn. My sampler suggests how you might begin yours.

When your zigzag lines are worked in reverse to the ones above, their peaks and valleys interlock to form diamond shapes. Fill the diamonds with contrasting thread, color, and stitch.

72

Diamonds, hearts, scallops, fish scales, hexagons, and ogees will develop as you freely arrange your stitches and rows. When you do zigzag or flame patterns, work one row as a guideline. When you make a hexagon, you should set the whole motif and center the design in the middle of your canvas.

Color can make Florentine work glorious. Traditionally, five or more finely graduated shades of one color were used before a new color was introduced. The colors were muted and soft. Blending and shading colors is still a goal worth aiming for, but today we are leaning toward a much more bold and brilliant palette. Abrupt changes of color and unexpected combinations introduce drama and vitality into Florentine design.

FLORENTINE SAMPLER

Another mini-sampler, this time exploring the design possibilities of the Florentine stitch. I used a variety of threads, and added an occasional bead or sequin to give the smooth Florentine stitches sparkle.

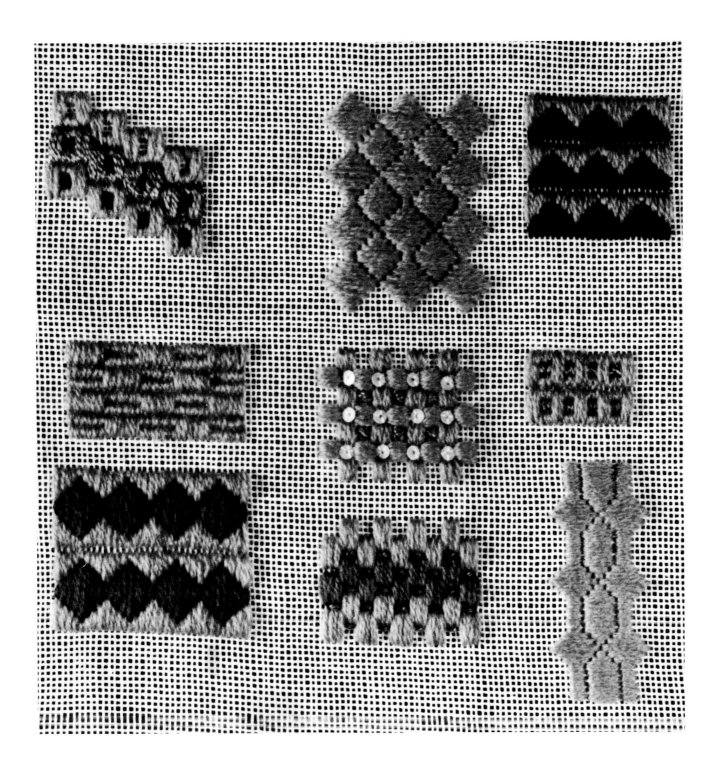

73

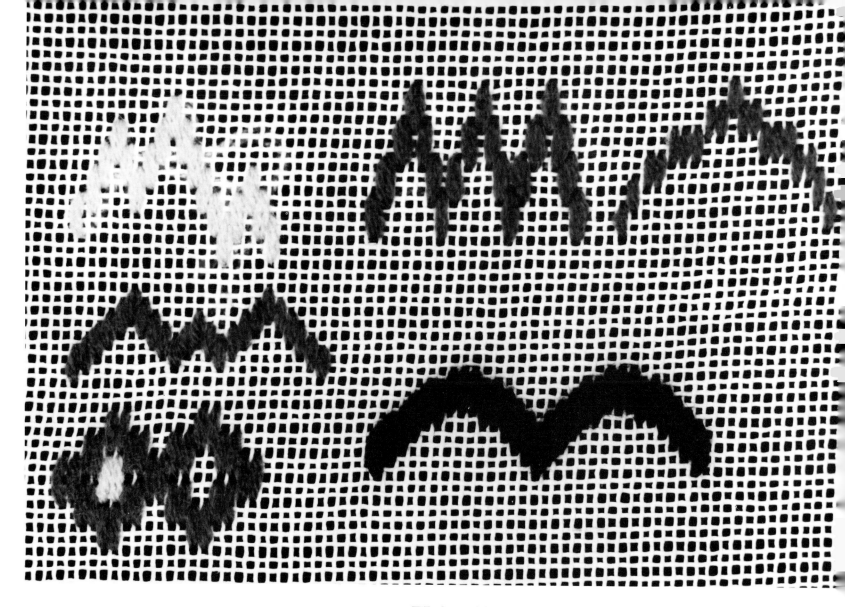

FLORENTINE SAMPLER

Florentine stitches worked in Persian yarn and pearl cotton thread are explored on Number 16 canvas. I used three shades of green, varying the length and steps of the stitches, grouping some, using others singly. This is another example of making a sampler that will serve as a learning experience and act as a memo of ideas tested.

FLORENTINE PAIRS

Pairs of Florentine stitches covering four canvas threads each climb up and down the canvas, two canvas threads at a time. Three strands of Persian yarn are used to ensure coverage of the Number 12 canvas. Under and over all the pairs of pink and white stitches, I backstitched a fuchsia metallic thread to highlight the design. (The backstitch is worked horizontally over two canvas threads.) Center the pattern by placing the top pair of stitches of a diamond in the center of the canvas.

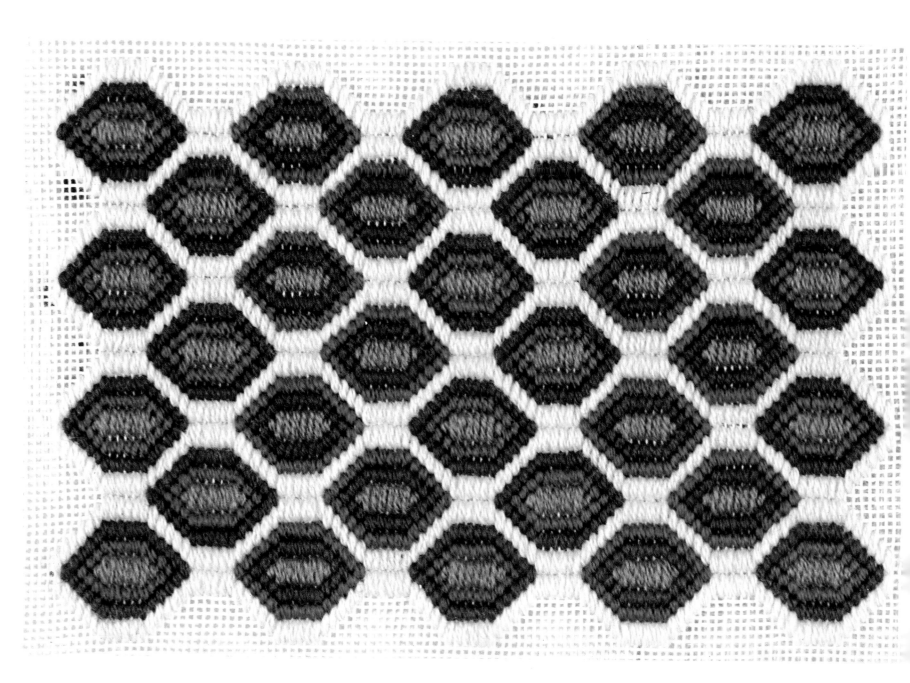

OGEE

This self-explanatory pattern in Florentine stitches of different lengths gets its variation through a subtle shift of position of the colors as well as through the long and short stitches. Center the design and work the entire framework, filling it in later. 1t is stitched on Number 12 canvas with the full strand of Persian yarn.

ARGYLE PLAID

The design is made up entirely of Florentine stitches worked over four threads of Number 16 canvas with two strands of Persian yarn. Each small diamond in the pattern consists of nine Florentine stitches. The large diamond results from a zigzag pattern in light beige. Center the large diamond outline to start the design and note that the stitches step up and down two canvas threads.

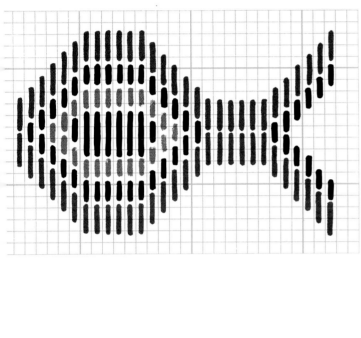

MINARETS

With two strands of Persian yarn on Number 16 canvas, work all stitches over four canvas threads stepping up and down two. The pattern flares out when you increase the number of stitches to a step at intervals, following singly worked stitches. Work a complete minaret in the center of the canvas and continue working the rest of the pattern, filling in as you go on later. Where the minarets interlock with one another, small diamonds emerge. Double diamonds mark the exact center of the minaret.

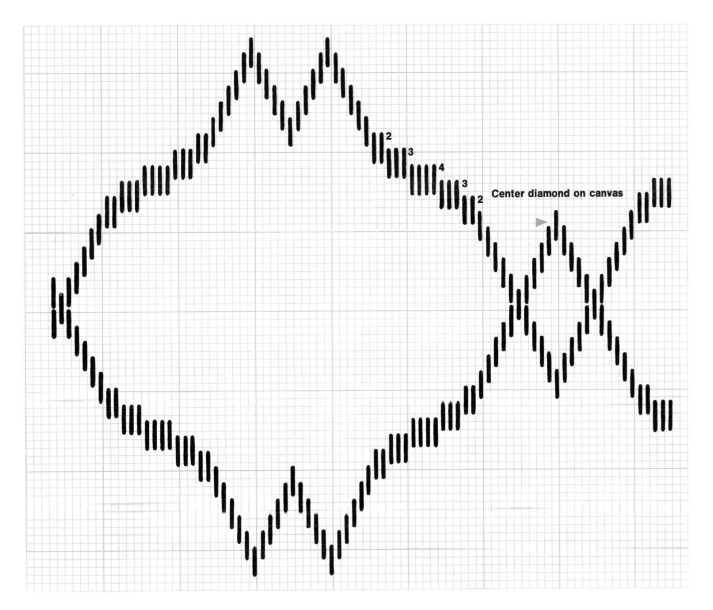

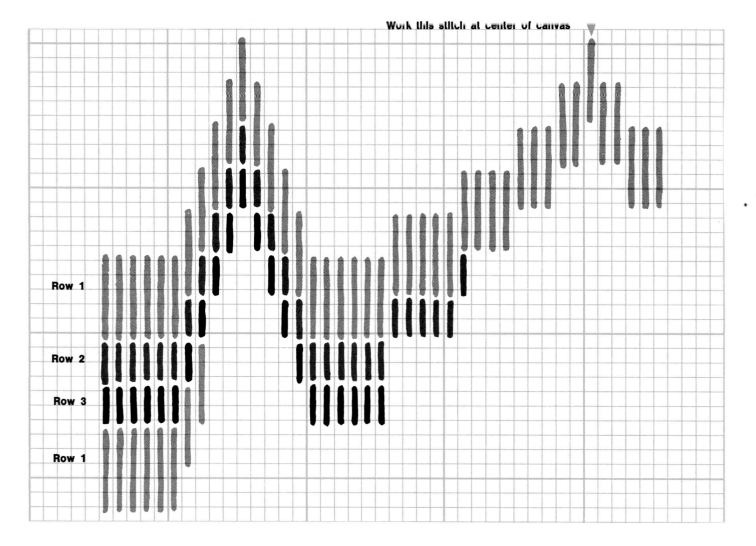

Work this stitch at center of canvas

Row 1

Row 2

Row 3

Row 1

FLORENTINE STEEPLES

Start the pattern in the center of the canvas with row 1 in white. The design requires three colors and is worked here on Number 12 canvas with the full strand of Persian yarn. Note how the length of the stitches varies and that there are as many as six stitches to a step. The pattern steps up and down three canvas threads. (The steps in a Florentine pattern represent how many horizontal threads of canvas, up or down, a new stitch extends beyond the last one. The higher the step, the steeper the angle. A series of one steps will produce a gradual, almost rounded look.)

80

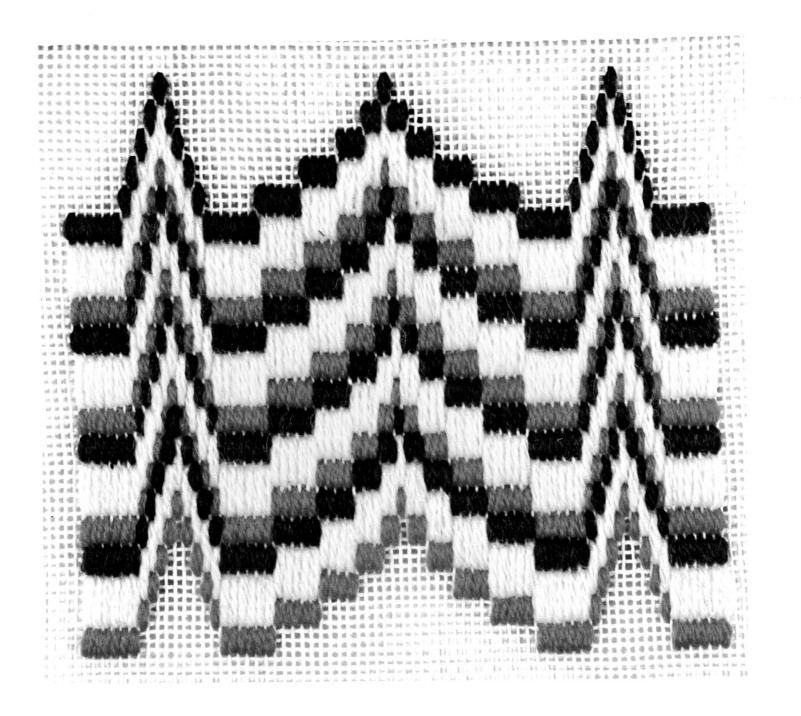

82

Pillow worked in the Florentine "gem" pattern in four colors in Persian yarn.

FLORENTINE GEMS

Start with a cross-stitch over three threads in the center of Number 16 canvas. Carefully following the diagram and photograph, work each of the four sides of a gem, North, West, South and East, turning the canvas a quarter turn each time. Use two strands of Persian yarn and fill in the centers of the gem in any way you choose. I decided on a green glass bead, but cross, tent, Smyrna or rice stitches are all possibilities. The gems are linked together with cross-stitches in a different color. Carefully watch the alternation of the gem colors. They are usually worked in two shades of two colors, but the design is equally exciting with four totally different colors.

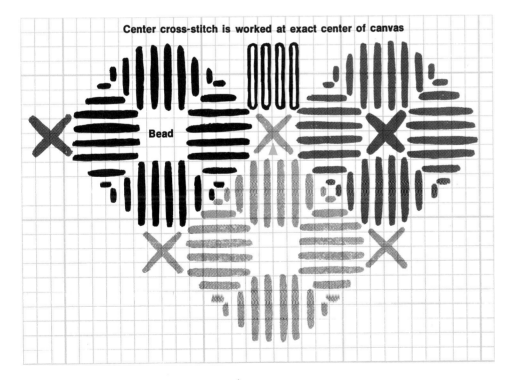

Center cross-stitch is worked at exact center of canvas

Bead

83

SPARKLING HONEYCOMB

The two long stitches in navy Persian yarn should be worked over the center of the canvas. Complete the outline of the honeycomb, returning to fill it in with other colors. Long and short stitches combine on Number 16 canvas with two strands of Persian yarn and metallic thread for sparkle and contrast. This pattern makes a stunning evening bag, or bolero for velvet pants, or slippers.

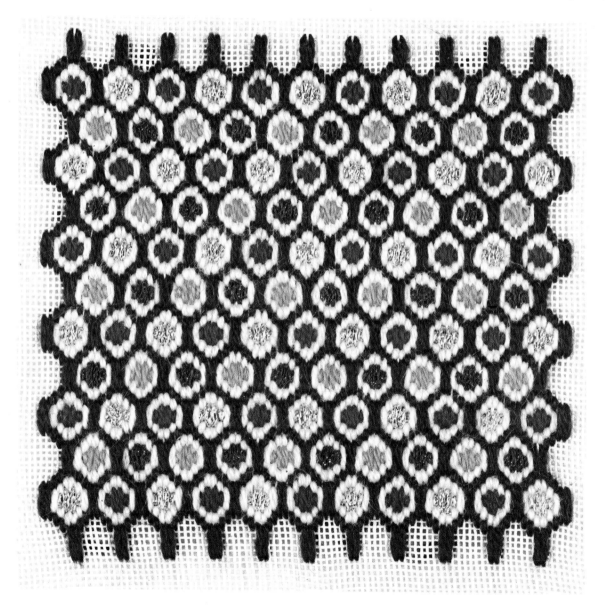

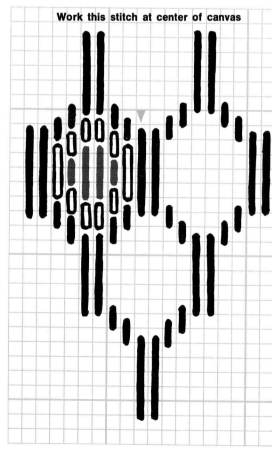

Work this stitch at center of canvas

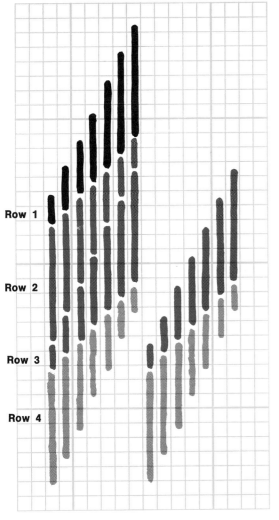

Row 1

Row 2

Row 3

Row 4

FLORENTINE SLIVERS

Slivers can be worked across the canvas with each color or in sections from the top down, setting in all four colors as you go. The pattern is worked as follows: in row 1, stitches are worked over two, three, four, five, six, seven, and then eight canvas threads consecutively, moving up *two* canvas threads; in row 2, reverse the order and work over eight, seven, six, five, four, three, and finally two threads, each stitch climbing up *one* canvas thread; in rows 3 and 4, repeat these two rows alternately from the top to the botom.

In the pattern shown here three strands of Persian yarn were used to cover Number 12 canvas. *(Design by Edith John.)*

FLORENTINE FIRELIGHT

While all the stitches are worked over six canvas threads, there are changes in the steps of the pattern. The peaks step up and down three canvas threads and there are stitches that step up and down one canvas thread causing a gradual flare out of the pattern. Look at the diagram carefully. The change in step creates a variation in texture while five shades of bittersweet give off a luminous shimmer of color. The design was worked on Number 12 canvas with three strands of Persian yarn for the sake of easy reading, though I prefer it on Number 16 canvas with two strands of yarn. Center the first row using it as a guideline for the entire pattern.

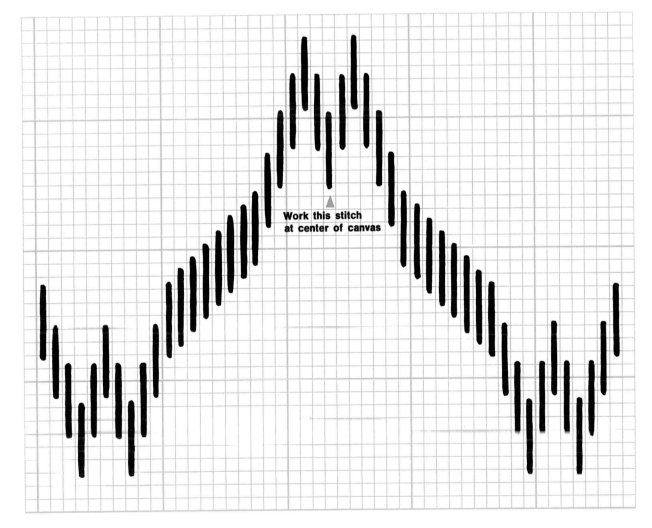

Work this stitch
at center of canvas

8 CROSSED STITCHES

THE CROSS-STITCH

The cross-stitch can be worked over anything from one to four canvas intersections. Make one diagonal stitch that crosses from lower right to upper left; then complete the cross with another diagonal stitch from lower left to upper right. Work a horizontal row from right to left, crossing each stitch as you go; all the top stitches in any row should slant in the same direction, from lower left to upper right. You can work cross-stitches in vertical or diagonal rows, as well, and in scattered squares throughout a design.

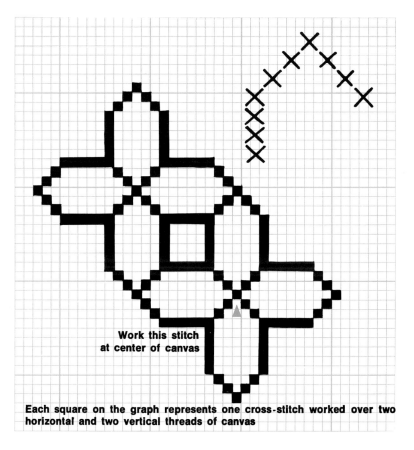

Work this stitch at center of canvas

Each square on the graph represents one cross-stitch worked over two horizontal and two vertical threads of canvas

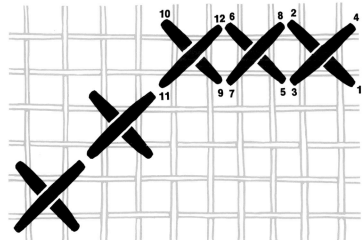

CROSS-STITCH STARS AND SQUARES

The cross-stitches are worked over two canvas threads. To start, work the two diagonal lines that crisscross over the exact center of the canvas. Continue working the cross-stitches that outline the shape of the star. Fill the inside of the star with the colors you prefer. Each star interlocks with those above, below, and alongside it—their points sharing one cross stitch. There are two stars of different colors, each shaded with its center in a contrasting row of color. The squares are also outlined in white and filled with two shades of a color. Three stars are pictured in various stages of development to make the working order clear. Use two strands of Persian yarn on Number 14 canvas.

THE SMYRNA OR DOUBLE CROSS-STITCH

The Smyrna stitch makes a neat, bulky mound. It works well on a mono canvas and doesn't snag at all, since there are four crossings of each stitch.

To make the Smyrna you do an ordinary cross-stitch and then put an upright cross on top of it. The upright cross can be worked in a second color. But whatever colors you use, the crossing sequence should be consistent.

The Smyrna can be worked over two, three, or four canvas threads. It can be arranged in horizontal, vertical, or diagonal rows. This stitch can also be scattered over your canvas for special textural effect in an otherwise flat area.

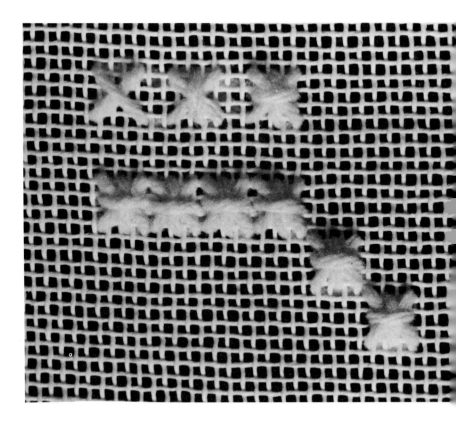

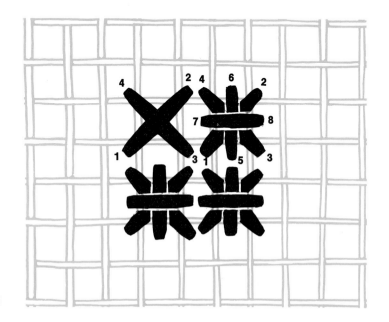

LARGE HOUNDSTOOTH CHECK

Smyrna stitch squares are worked over four canvas threads on Number 16 canvas. One Houndstooth Check is formed from eight Smyrna stitches. Center the first check and work the rest in vertical and horizontal rows according to the photograph. Watch the placement of color. To get a glint into the design, I backstitched around the brown check with brown metallic thread. This pattern makes a striking cummerbund on a smaller gauge canvas and a marvelous telephone book cover in any scale.

90

91

92

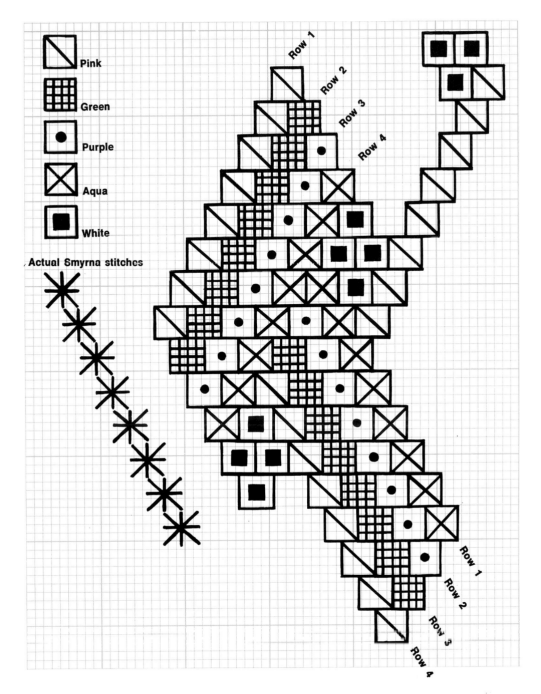

Legend

- Pink
- Green
- Purple
- Aqua
- White

Actual Smyrna stitches

Row 1
Row 2
Row 3
Row 4

Row 1
Row 2
Row 3
Row 4

SMYRNA RIBBON

Four colors weave over and under each other in a basket-weave pattern which takes on a pointillist look when it is done in Smyrna stitches. Eight stitches per color and thirty-two stitches in all compose a ribbon. Moving up and down the canvas in a gradual slope, each new stitch steps over two *vertical* canvas threads and down four while the *upper* left to lower right diagonal cross of the stitch is started in the center mesh of the base of the stitch above it. (This is most important in understanding the way each stitch moves outward and down.) The Smyrna stitches in this pattern are worked over four canvas threads on Number 16 canvas with three strands of Persian yarn.

THE RICE STITCH

The rice stitch is also called the crossed corners stitch because it is an ordinary cross-stitch with each of its four corners or arms crossed by a diagonal top stitch. The rice stitch can be worked over two, three, or four canvas threads in horizontal, vertical, or diagonal rows. You must complete all the crossings before you go on to the next stitch, but the order in which you work it doesn't matter.

You can vary this pattern by working all your crosses separately and then returning to cross all the corners with a different thread or color.

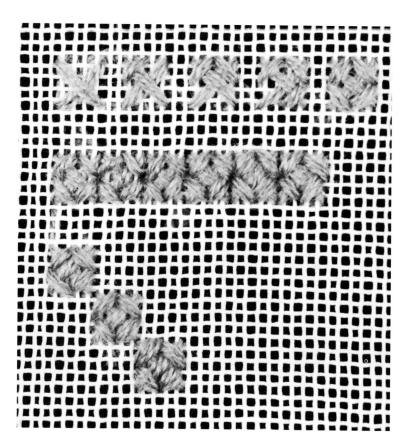

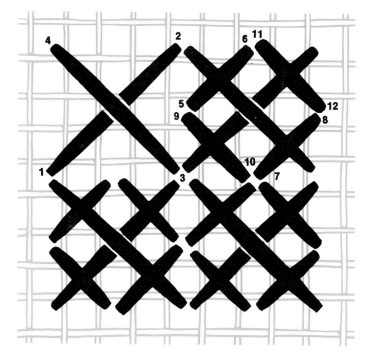

Try building this stitch on an upright cross over eight canvas threads. Cross the corners with vertical and horizontal stitches. Make sure your yarn is thick enough to cover the canvas. You can alternate rows of light and dark color and the result is a dramatic, striped pattern of upright rice stitches —the rice stitch "straight up."

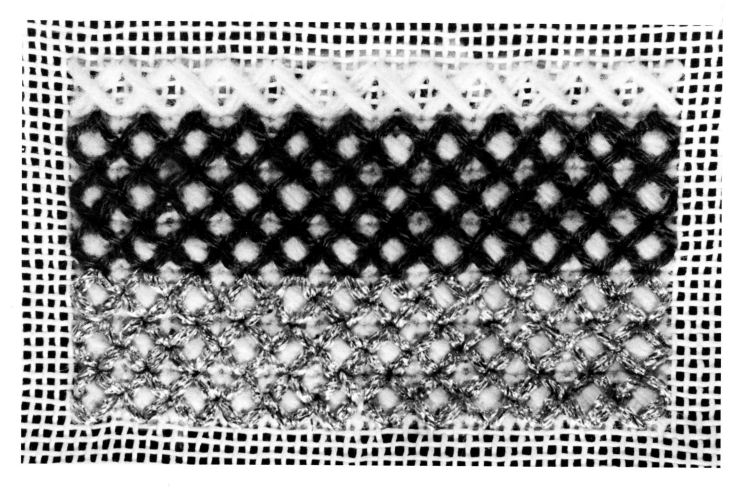

RICE STITCH
Variation Number 1

The variation is begun by making a cross-stitch in a thread of your own choice, in this case Persian yarn. The ordinary cross-stitch has its corners crossed here with a lustrous rayon thread in a contrasting color, or with gold thread. In each instance, the surface threads, or the thread used to cross the corners will dominate.

RICE RIBBON

Four shades of beige ribbon weave under four shades of bittersweet ribbon in this version of the basketweave pattern. There are thirty-two rice stitches per color, eight to a shade. The ribbons are worked diagonally down the canvas in a gradual slope, each new rice stitch moving over two vertical canvas threads and down four while *the upper left to lower right diagonal cross of the stitch is started in the center mesh of the base of the stitch above it.* (This is critical in achieving the slanted steps which make the design.) Each stitch interlocks with the one before it and is worked over four threads of canvas. Three strands of Persian yarn are used to cover Number 16 canvas. The group of four black Smyrna stitches separate the ribbons on facing page.

SHADED SCALLOPS

Each square represents one rice stitch worked over four canvas threads. Use three strands of Persian yarn on Number 16 canvas. The pattern is simply a matter of working rows of rice stitches horizontally, vertically, and diagonally. There are five closely graded shades of salmon, two shades of olive green, and a dark brown for the outlining—which I suggest be done first. The middle stitch of the three Smyrna stitches at the center of the scallop stem should be worked over the center of your canvas. Once the outline is completed, it acts as a guideline for the rest of the design. The continuation of the brown outline rows indicates the beginnings of other scallops. The base of one scallop is the keystone of the one beneath it. The shading goes from dark outside to light at the center but can be reversed and even alternated from motif to motif. A very durable fabric due to the many crossings of wool thread, this pattern makes a hardy and beautiful rug. It is scaled larger by choosing larger canvas and, of course, thickening the thread. (See the chair covered with a *scallops* pattern worked in cross-stitch over two canvas threads on Number 14 canvas, page 8.) The chair cushion is an example of variation both in texture and scale of one design idea. In simple words—same pattern, different stitch and over smaller area.

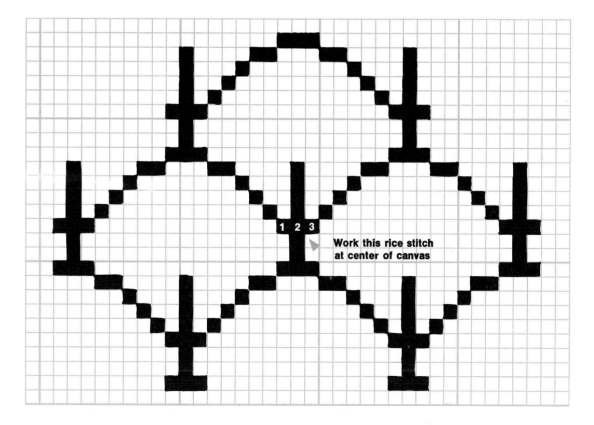

1 2 3

Work this rice stitch at center of canvas

98

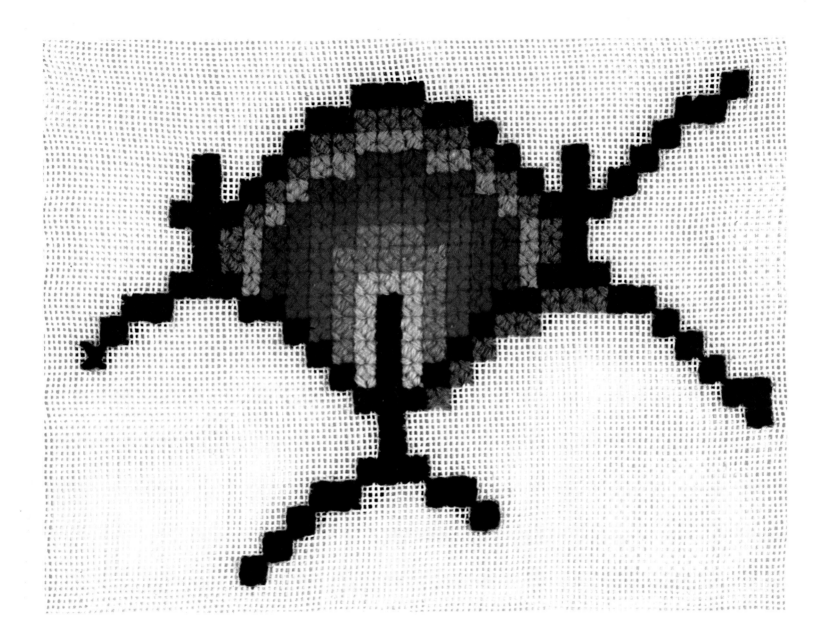

DIAMOND STRIPE

The simple repetition of Florentine stitches worked over four canvas threads, stepping up and down two canvas threads, resulted in this unusual textured stripe design. There are eight groups or blocks of stitches to a diamond, four to each step. The centers of the diamonds are filled with Rhodes stitches in silver thread. Three threads of Persian yarn were used to cover Number 12 canvas. Note the textural contrasts between the smooth, long Florentine stitches and the chunky, squared Rhodes stitch in metallic thread. This design is another variation on the theme of the stripe, an age-old design form.

9 SPECIAL EFFECTS STITCHES

All embroidery stitches are meant to embellish a canvas, but the stitches I call "special effects" stitches will give you something truly special. Because of size, shape, or texture, these stitches add an extraordinary decorative dimension to your design.

THE RHODES STITCH

The Rhodes stitch begins with a long diagonal stitch from upper right to lower left, and, when completed, makes a bold, raised, textured square. Rhodes stitches can be worked in horizontal, vertical, and diagonal rows, and they can be combined with other stitches as well. But no matter which way you work the rows, the crossing sequence for each stitch must be followed carefully.

The diagram shows three stages in making the Rhodes stitch. Study each stage before you work the stitch. In the diagram, this stitch is made over twenty-four canvas threads. But as you can see from the design, this high-rise square can be even larger.

You can vary this stitch by working it to the halfway point where it looks like an hourglass. Fill in around each hourglass with tent stitches.

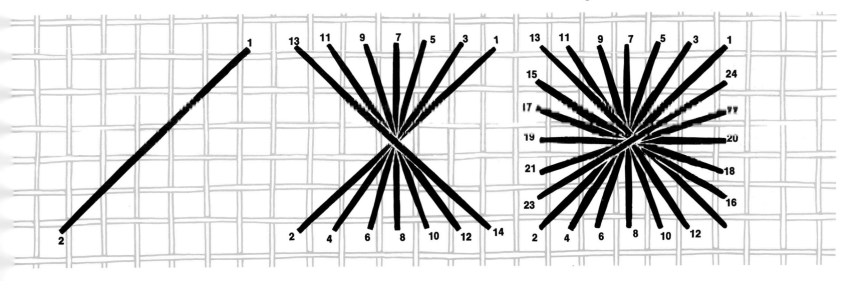

RHODES STITCH DESIGN

The Rhodes stitch, in combination with the basketweave stitch, is worked in a rising and falling checkerboard pattern on Number 10 canvas with three strands of Persian yarn. To vary the design in a special way, work large cross-stitches in gold thread across a few random black basketweave squares. The Rhodes stitch is worked over twenty-eight threads of canvas and there are forty-nine stitches to a square of basketweave stitches. To begin, find the center stitch of any square and work it in the center of the canvas. The high and low relief is an important feature of the pattern.

SQUARE MEDLEY

Squares of tent, Rhodes and scattered Gobelin stitches combine in this variation of the checkerboard. The design was worked on Number 12 canvas with two strands of Persian yarn. The satin stitches were worked on top of existing needlepoint to accent random squares.

LOZENGES

Different length stitches form a lozenge motif across the canvas with a Rhodes stitch in the center to provide a change of texture. The pattern is worked on Number 12 canvas with three strands of Persian yarn. Center the pattern by working a long red stitch in the center of the canvas.

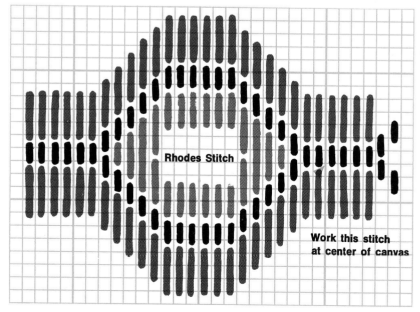

Rhodes Stitch

Work this stitch at center of canvas

SHADED LEAVES

Leaf stitches are arranged in horizontal rows of shaded colors on Number 12 canvas. The five colors are repeated every five rows, but the shades are arranged in reverse order. Use two strands of wool yarn. The vein at the base of each leaf is optional.

THE LEAF STITCH

The leaf stitch is composed of twelve tilted Gobelin stitches that radiate out from a central "stalk," assuming the shape of veins in a leaf. It creates a very textured surface and must be worked with great care so you don't miss a mesh or go into the same mesh twice. Make sure, however, to skip one mesh under the first stitch. You can work one side first, then the other, although in the diagram I have indicated that it is worked in a clockwise direction from the topmost stitch.

A central vein consisting of one vertical stitch (the twelfth stitch) over three canvas threads may be added at the base of the leaf.

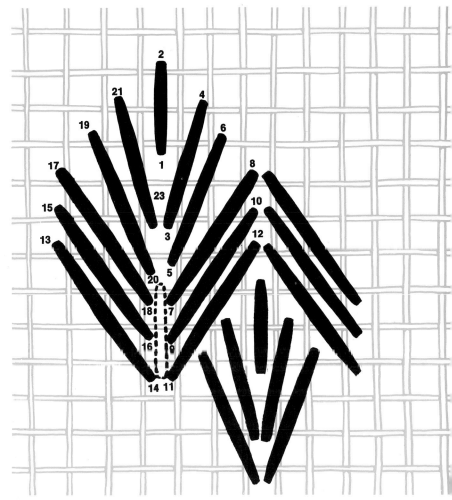

FOUR QUARTER LEAVES

This design is based on a division of the canvas into four quarters defined by diagonal lines from upper left to lower right and from lower left to upper right. Dot the top of each canvas intersection all the way up and down with light pencil marks to outline the diagonal edges or corners of each quarter. The lines will meet and cross at the center of the canvas where the first leaf stitch should be worked. Turn the canvas to work the second, third and fourth leaves. Each step suggests the next. Don't panic at the gaps that evolve between leaves. Fill them as the power of invention moves you after you have completed the surrounding pattern of leaves, as I have done here. Work the pattern in all four quarters, not just one, so that there is continuity and you can see quickly how each quarter dovetails with the others at the diagonal edges. Notice how the third row of leaf stitches joins at the corners where the row turns.

THE DIAMOND EYELET STITCH

The diamond eyelet is a multiple stitch made up of sixteen stitches that radiate from the same center mesh. This means that the yarn goes through the center again and again.

The stitches forming the points of the diamond are worked over four threads, those in between over three, then two, then three. The outside edge of the stitch assumes the shape of a diamond.

Your yarn should be neither too thick nor too thin to execute this stitch: if it is too thick, it will not go through the center all those times, and if it is too thin, the canvas will show through around the spokes. Experiment with different yarns to find the right thickness for your canvas.

THE DIAMOND EYELET STITCH

This exceptionally decorative stitch works well as a filler and is also quite capable of standing alone and creating an interesting pattern. When the entire design is finished, an optional outline of backstitches can be stitched around the diamonds in a different thread, color, or stitch. I chose to use a backstitch in fuchsia metallic thread. French knots filling in around the diamonds create still another variation and some extra texture.

Begin by bringing your needle and thread out of the mesh that marks the center of the canvas. Work the stitch according to directions. All the rest of the pattern grows out from this first stitch which interlocks with those above, beneath and beside it.

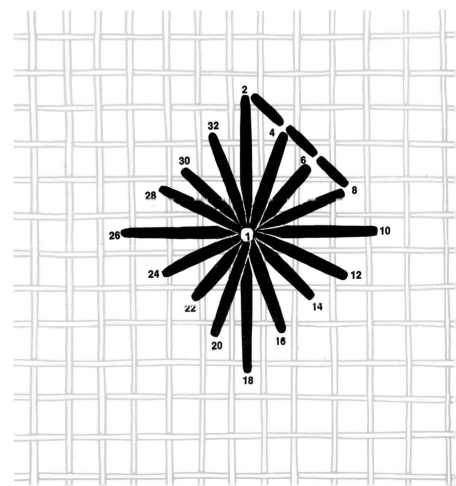

SILVER DIAMONDS

The diamond eyelet stitch has a quilted or tufted look when it is worked between rows of smooth Florentine stitches.

Center and stitch a zigzag row of Florentine stitches. Work the next zigzag row in reverse to it and notice that where their points touch, diamond shapes form. Fill these shapes with diamond eyelet stitches in silver thread. Give them an extra textural touch by topping them with French knots in a completely different color. The pattern was worked on Number 12 canvas with three threads of Persian yarn, two strands of silver thread, and for the French knot, rayon or cotton.

THE FOUR-SIDED STITCH

Straight stitches, both vertical and horizontal, are used to form the square that makes this stitch. The outside of the square covers seven canvas threads per side. The next row inside covers five threads of canvas per side. The next row covers three threads per side, and the last row covers one.

You can work this square in any direction at all. Each new square is started one thread next to the last square above, below, or beside it.

There are many ways to vary the four-sided stitch. You can use a contrasting thread, a bead, or a button at the center of each square. Or you can repeat four different colors from the outside to the center of each square. Your squares can be worked in solid colors and you can alternate the color by rows. You can even alternate rows with different kinds of yarn.

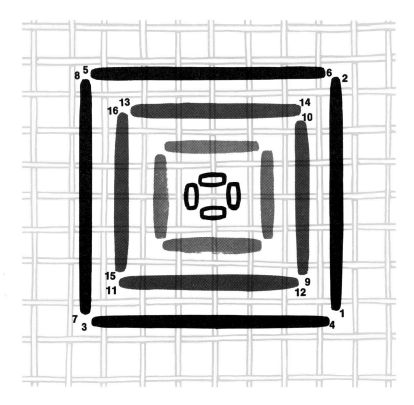

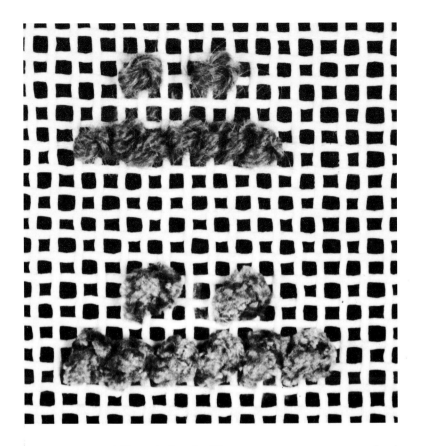

Two groups of French knots. The upper group was worked in Persian yarn, the lower one in chenille.

THE FRENCH KNOT

The French knot is a very old embroidery stitch. In needlepoint it can be worked alone or in clusters for special effects. It can be arranged in rows going in any direction, or it can be used to fill areas of a pattern.

You can work this stitch on bare canvas or you can work it over existing needlepoint; it creates a rough, pebbled surface, one you can't resist touching. But then, texture is the *raison d'être* of the French knot.

The French knot is like a tent stitch—only the yarn is twisted around the needle topside before the needle is inserted in the canvas again. Follow the diagram, securing the yarn on the underside of the canvas if you are only making one knot.

Fascinating fat French knots can be worked in rows of chenille yarn, and make an unusual pattern when alternated with rows of Gobelin stitches in Persian wool yarn.

FRENCH KNOTS

The thread is brought up through the hole or mesh (1) in the canvas where the knot is to be worked. This thread is then held taut with the left hand during the whole of the operation. The needle is placed behind the thread and is then turned around it so that the thread is wrapped *once* around the needle. Continue to turn the needle in a clockwise direction until it can be inserted through a mesh in the canvas next to the one through which the thread first emerged. The thread is then pulled tight as the tension is gradually released by the left hand. The needle should not be taken down through the same hole as the one through which it had originally emerged unless the thread is very thick and would not be in danger of being pulled right through to the back of the work. This diagram indicates the knot going over one intersection of canvas threads, from lower left to upper right. *(Diagram by Mary Rhodes.)*

10 DO'S AND DON'TS

DO'S, BEFORE YOU START

Buy the very best quality of all materials.

Buy an extra generous supply of yarn to avoid matching problems.

Test durability of novelty threads.

Leave a two- or three-inch margin around the entire canvas.

Bind the cut edges of canvas to check raveling.

Test marking pens.

DO'S, AS YOU WORK

Use waterproof pens or india ink for marking.

Use a hard lead pencil for defining the center and margins.

Mark the top of the canvas.

Count threads, not meshes.

Select colors in daylight, and do intricate shading by daylight.

Choose correct needle size.

Keep your working thread about eighteen to twenty inches long.

Center the first motif—most of the time.

Add beads, jewels, and so on, after blocking but before mounting.

Be sure that the threads cover the canvas.

Keep tent stitches going in the same direction.

Keep your place by leaving the needle in the middle of a row, stationed in the mesh.

Remember you can use tent stitches to fill in gaps between larger stitches.

Discard yarn that isn't fresh or has fluffed or thinned.

Maintain even, relaxed tension.

Work all threads almost two or three inches from the end; don't waste thread.

Weave end of thread under about ten stitches to secure it.

Use shorter lengths when using fragile threads like the metallics.

To rip, unthread the needle, lift, and remove unwanted stitches with the tip of needle.

If scissors are used, take care not to snip the canvas.

Sign and date work unobtrusively.

Work three extra rows of stitches around all sides of the needlepoint for seam allowance (more—two inches—for framing a picture).

Fold, roll, or crush canvas for most comfortable working position.

Check finished work for any stitches that have been left out and fill in. This is easily done with magnifying glass.

Finish off thread ends in different directions to avoid ridges topside.

Work colored ends into the completed stitches of same color. Sometimes, a dark end woven through the back of light-colored stitches will create a shadow on the surface.

Work the ends into stitches of the same color to avoid disturbing stitches of another color should you need to snip out an area later.

Put aside a few strands of each color and shade in case you want to buy more yarn. It is easier to match strands than worked color areas.

DON'TS

Don't:

make knots.

stitch to the edge of the canvas; work only to the margin line.

split threads when stitching.

allow working thread to twist. Stop and allow it to hang out.

re-use pulled out threads; discard them.

leave long ends of yarn on underside; secure them well and clip them close.

use too many stitches, colors, or textures in one design.

choose long, loose, and snaggy stitches for rugs and seat cushions.

start a pattern before a trial run on a sampler.

use canvas with weak, uneven, or knotted threads.

carry long threads on the back of your work that link up with other shapes. They pull and pucker the surface. Better to end and begin again.

11 BLOCKING

Blocking will smooth out and straighten finished needlepoint that may have stretched or pulled out of shape during the stitching. The margin of about two inches of extra canvas that was included in your original measurement of materials will be very useful now. Never cut the extra canvas; leave margins and edges intact as a place to put the tacks. Never tack into worked needlepoint.

To remove any soil picked up from handling, dip the needlepoint into cold water and Ivory Liquid—never use a detergent. Rinse thoroughly in cool water, but do not wring the needlepoint. Simply roll it in a dry towel to blot up most of the excess rinse water. There will be no bleeding or running of color if you used permanent markers for the guidelines on your canvas. Don't panic if, after you wet your finished needlepoint, it feels like a limp rag. The starch in the canvas has been dissolved and the stiffness has momentarily gone out of it. Once it is dry, the needlepoint reassumes not only its shape but its original stiff body.

BLOCKING EQUIPMENT

Rustproof push-pins.
Drawing or insulation board, Homosote.
Aluminum foil paper.
T-square.
Ivory Liquid soap.
Ruler.

Unroll the damp needlepoint and place it face up on a board covered with aluminum foil. I find that half-inch insulation board is best for this, as pins pierce it easily and yet stay firmly in place. But you can use a wooden drawing board or whatever suits you. Tack each of the corners of your canvas to the board with a rustproof push-pin; then, using a T-square or a straight-edge to be certain that the piece is truly straight, carefully pull and stretch each section of the needlework into shape, securing the edges with pins placed about one inch apart. The pins must often be moved several times as you tighten and adjust the canvas. Many people find blocking, with all its pulling and stretching, quite hard on the fingers.

When you are satisfied that everything is square and smooth, leave the needlepoint to dry completely—even if it takes several days.

The masking tape used to bind the edges tends to loosen somewhat in the wetting of the canvas. I usually leave it alone, trimming loose pieces. This is another good reason for having a two-inch margin on your canvas—even if a row or two do unravel, the worked needlepoint is unaffected and protected.

If you are afraid that immersing finished needlepoint in water might cause a permanent loss of body, or even color bleeding, try the blocking method I recently used for mixed-media stitchery. Dampen the entire piece of work with a moist sponge or cloth; then stretch, true it, and tack it into shape on your blocking board.

12 MOUNTING

Mounting is the term used to describe the way that needlepoint is finished or applied to an article or object. For the best results use the most professional help you can find for the mounting and finishing of completed needlepoint articles. You can put pillows, doorstops, or framed pieces together yourself. Most people, unless they are very handy with small tools and the sewing machine, find it safer to entrust their work to professionals. Leather-trimmed articles, telephone books, boxes, address books, tennis racket covers, wallets, checkbook covers, belts, handbags, wastebaskets, and other similar pieces should be sent to firms with long experience in this kind of work. The names and addresses of several of these sources are provided on page 145. I've found these firms to be completely reliable as long as you provide them with full instructions and complete information.

All canvases sent to the mounter should have the top designated so that designs are turned the right way when finished.

I pack my needlepoint in large manila envelopes and send it via insured first class mail. It usually takes three or four weeks to be mounted. Mounting is quite expensive, especially for leather items; it costs about twenty-five dollars for an address book, and forty dollars for a telephone book, although there is some variation between dealers, and between the rates they charge for wholesale as opposed to retail customers. Blocking first at home saves a few dollars. Some mounters, however, prefer to do the blocking themselves.

The mounter uses the leather that you choose to match a telephone book needlepoint cover, for example. He matches both with moiré or faille. The needlepoint is then blocked (if it hasn't been already), backed with leather, and lined with moiré or faille to match. If the piece requires tiny hardware, such as a rod to keep a telephone book cover firmly attached to the book, rings for a loose-leaf address book, gold knobs for a handbag bottom, a handbag chain, or a handbag clasp, it is added in the process.

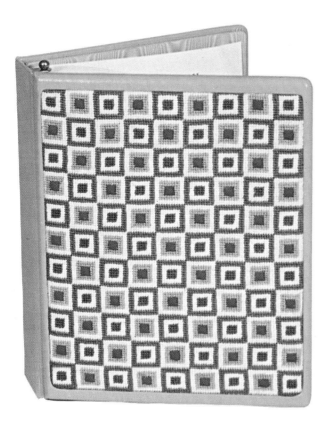

Telephone book cover worked in optical squares pattern of tent and Rhodes stitches, and mounted in leather to match. (Worked by Mrs. Henry Adler.)

PART III